THE QUIET STRENGTH OF RESILIENCE

A Holocaust Survival Story Spanning Four Generations

By

Ron Schwarz

ISBN (Hardccover): 979-8-9923597-0-1

ISBN (Paperback): 979-8-9923597-1-8

Printed in USA

This book is dedicated to my father, Charles Schwarz, who taught me how to bounce forward. I miss him!

Praise for The Quiet Strength of Resilience

This is a very powerful, beautifully written book. Ron is a wonderful storyteller, and the tale is so very moving. He not only knows his history, but he also knows how to breathe a human soul into that history.

Dr. David Patterson, University of Texas at Dallas
Hillel Feinberg Distinguished Chair in Holocaust Studies

The harrowing story of a son's quest to understand his father's childhood experience as a Jewish refugee in Europe during World War II, The Quiet Strength of Resilience is equally a heart-warming story of filial affection and admiration—of the unique yet universal ties that bind families together during periods of extraordinary struggle, and across generations. Ron Schwarz is right: the more people have a chance to read stories like his and his father's, the more inclined they might be to stand up to antisemitism and see "the quiet strength of resilience" in others.

Dr. Adam Nelson, Senior Associate Dean
School of Education, University of Wisconsin

Captivating. Moving. Gut wrenching. Humorous. Brave. These are some of the words that ran through my head after knowing this story. This is an unbelievable story to pass on to the generations. We can never let that happen again!

Stephen Robinson, Truist Wealth Management

This book is unique in the perils felt and the persistence to push forward that were pursued by Ron's father. Unlike other survivor stories, this book adds the unique perspective of the next generation's journey to preserve history by putting all the parts of stories shared together and also trying to perceive how their parent survivor must have felt. Ron passionately researched and traveled throughout Europe to substantiate with documents his father's journey. Ron makes the history personal so that it resonates with the reader. He has honored his father by sharing his story and is also combatting antisemitism at the same time.

Stacy Singerman, Chief Operating Officer, The Macula Society

TABLE OF CONTENTS

A NOTE

While I have taken great pains to ensure the accuracy of the events in this book, some gaps inevitably appeared. And although my father was glad to give me factual accounts, he tended to avoid expressing his thoughts and feelings during those tumultuous days and years. It's easy to understand why he tried to avoid reliving those feelings of abandonment, loneliness, fear, and grief.

Given the common thread of human emotions, I have sometimes surmised how he must have felt. I have filled in missing pieces as accurately as I can, extrapolating from my knowledge and research of many accounts of those days.

Aside from those assumptions, this story entirely is true.

INTRODUCTION

There are a million or more Holocaust survival stories. They are all worth telling. They are all important.

I believe this one is especially critical, not only for what it will tell you about my family but for what it means in the world right now.

The number of hate crimes against Jews is staggering and has been growing in recent years. The United States Department of Justice and The Southern Poverty Law Center reported that hate crimes against Jews have risen about four hundred percent since 2017. Since the October 7, 2023 attack in Israel, they've skyrocketed even more.

Hate has found a voice and platform in America.

Perhaps it would not have found such an easy foothold if younger people knew about stories like my father's. Research says that people who know about the Holocaust are far less likely to be antisemitic.

Dr. Aliza S. Wong, a history professor at Texas Tech University in Lubbock, presented research showing that thirty-two percent of millennials in America have never heard of the Holocaust, while a staggering sixty-five percent have never heard of Auschwitz.

I regularly give presentations to school groups at the Dallas Holocaust and Human Rights Museum. Most are not Social Studies classes – they are English students doing units on prejudice and intolerance. Unfortunately, teaching the Holocaust doesn't fit neatly into the public school curricula.

I don't believe you have to be a Jew to know that teaching about the Holocaust is crucial. I want this book to open people's eyes and minds.

I want to create change. With this book, I am endeavoring to do my part to eliminate antisemitism.

The Holocaust wasn't the first genocide in the history of the world, but it was of a scale never before imagined. For that reason alone, it's a piece of history that has to be taught. And it isn't old history. The barbarism of Auschwitz, gas chambers, torture, and mass graves didn't happen in the Dark Ages – it occurred during my father's time, and during my grandparents' time. It's recent.

Genocide is never okay, but in our Western culture, we seem to be more disconnected from places like Rwanda where the Hutus slaughtered the Tutsis, than we are from people who look more like us and whose culture feels familiar. The Holocaust took place in Europe, perpetrated by people who were an awful lot like us – people who were educated, wore suits and ties, drank fine wine, played with their children in the park, listened to Mozart, and commuted to work every day.

We hope that by teaching history, it won't repeat. Jews say, "Never again!" Every Jew lives with the question, "Could it happen again? Could it happen here?" It may not be a conscious thought that follows us through our days, but it lurks in the shadows – and we wonder.

One of the most devastating aspects of the October 7, 2023 attack in Israel was that Hamas borrowed terror strategies from the Nazi playbook. Their message screamed out, "Yes, it can happen again. It's happening now."

I always believed it could never happen again – and certainly, never happen here in America. But in 2017, when I saw that hate suddenly had a platform and was spewing out antisemitic rhetoric, I wasn't so sure anymore that it couldn't happen again – and happen here.

I grew up with my father's story. I remember when I was a child of eight, sitting in the passenger seat while my dad drove to his parent's house for Sunday lunch. During the forty-minute rides there and back, I'd pester him, "Dad, tell me that story again."

He always smiled, nodded, and told his story again and again until I knew it by heart. His story became mine and then evolved into the now unabridged version with all knowledge I uncovered through the research I've done.

We wear different hats as we go through life. I'm a boyfriend, a business owner, a dad, and, very importantly, the son of a Holocaust survivor. It's an identity I grew up with in a predominantly Jewish neighborhood in New York. My father was the only Holocaust survivor there, and I took a kind of pride in that. His experience set him and me apart. My father survived hardships I couldn't imagine. He was brave and strong. He gave me an identity that is an integral part of who I am today.

My father was a pretty stoic guy. When he told his stories, he matter-of-factly recounted events, but he also told me that when he first got to France, alone at age thirteen, he cried himself to sleep at night. He didn't tell me how many nights. I suspect it was quite a few.

I used to tell my father's story because I knew it so well, but it wasn't until I started gathering documents that offered solid proof of everything he had experienced, that it became real. Hearing it as a child, it had seemed more like a fable than real life. But here it was – the proof.

When I present his story now, complete with a PowerPoint presentation and many pages of original documents from the 1920s, 30s, and 40s, I believe I am honoring him, and he deserves that.

I began presenting at the Dallas Holocaust and Human Rights Museum in about 2016 when the museum started looking for second-generation survivors to fill the gaps of the original survivors who were too old to continue. I accepted an invitation to meet with Charlotte Decoster, the Ackerman Family Director of Education.

"Tell me your father's story," she said.

When I finished talking, she said, "Wait here." Several minutes later, she came back, carrying a thick manuscript that she placed on the table and opened to a specific page. She explained that the manuscript was her Ph.D. dissertation on Child Rescue as Survival Resistance: Hidden Children in Nazi-Occupied Western Europe. The page she pointed me to was an interview with a man named Georges Loigner. He talked about saving a large group of Jewish children from Germany who he spirited out of the country and moved around to safe places. He mentioned names of schools, and other locations in France – the exact path my father had taken.

I said, "Holy s**t, Charlotte! This is the guy that contacted my grandmother and got my father out of Germany!" That started me on a deep dive of investigation that led me to Germany, France, and Switzerland. I started with my biological grandfather who had been murdered in his jewelry store in Ludwigshafen. Certain that it would have been reported in the local newspaper, I contacted the city's municipal archives, giving them the event and the approximate date. The director of the archives sent me the newspaper article, but that was only the beginning.

"I got interested in your family's story," he said. "Come to Germany. Let's meet. I found a whole group of documents I'd like to share with you."

When I arrived, he revealed a treasure trove of papers confirming that the stories my father had told me were true – not the fables I had listened to with spellbound awe as a child. There were also seemingly endless documents about my grandparents who I knew, but about whose history and experience during the war, I had little knowledge.

Excited, I asked more questions. A graduate student at the University of Texas at Dallas helped me contact the Swiss authorities who uncovered another stack of eighty-nine papers documenting my father's time in Switzerland.

Lastly, I traveled to the Memorial de la Shoah, a Holocaust Museum in Paris. At the fourth-floor research center, I retrieved another handful of documents dealing with my father's life in France. My father hadn't known the details of his time there, that is, who was paying for his clothes, his housing and his support. I'm sure that was by design so that if any child was picked up by the Germans, they wouldn't be able to tell them much. These papers filled important gaps in my father's story.

While I was talking with one of the research librarians, another visitor overhead and said, "I heard your father lived in Clermont-Ferrand."

"Yes, for a little while."

"There's a historian there who knows everything about Clermont-Ferrand. He's not a Holocaust researcher but a historian specializing in Clermont-Ferrand. His name is Jean-Michel Ralliere and you should contact him."

After a quick flurry of emails, I discovered that Mr. Ralliere knew about my father. He also told me about Bernard Delpal, a historian specializing in Dieulefit where my father lived for a short time. He, too, knew a little bit about my father and his time in Dieulefit. Coincidence, or something more universal, was working in my favor. The German poet, Goethe wrote, "The moment one truly commits, serendipity moves too." It certainly did for me.

I've told these events you're about to read many times. People have told me it's a great story. I know it's an important one. My father never spent time in a concentration camp. My grandfather was imprisoned in Dachau, but only for a short time before the war. The accounts from the camps are critically important to know. They are haunting, horrific, and heart-rending. The fact that anyone survived is beyond comprehension.

But the Jews who were disenfranchised from their homeland, stripped of all their rights, and bereft of their homes and possessions

– their stories are equally worth telling. Every survivor's story is important. Each one merits a place in history. What happened to the Jews who escaped the camps was often devastating. Certainly, their lives would never be the same.

So many children were separated from their parents, never knowing if they would see them again, and never knowing if they would live or die from one day to the next.

I hope this book makes a difference to you. I hope what I've written will help you understand the full horror of genocide. I hope it changes your emotional state. I want you to feel what happened to my father deeply enough that you too will say, "Never again!"

Chapter 1

ESCAPE

March 12, 1939.

The school bell dismissed the students shortly after three p.m. Karl Schwarz walked back from his desk to the cloakroom, shrugged into his heavy woolen jacket, and slung his brown leather rucksack onto his back. Hooking his hands through the straps he walked down the hall and into the schoolyard, almost inured by now to the boys giving him a wide berth and sideways glances. A couple hollered after him as he passed, "Judenschwein (Jew pig)!"

He kept his head down. Best to make himself invisible. He knew what would happen if he fought back. His father had already been incarcerated in Dachau and released, his business taken away from him. Being a Jew meant you walked the streets with trepidation, cautious of every stranger coming your way.

Karl hurried home, turned into Prinzregentenstrasse, opened the heavy wooden door of the apartment building at the end of the block at number sixty-five, and climbed the steps to the second floor. He dropped his rucksack in the narrow hallway, hung his jacket on the hook, and walked into the kitchen, enticed by the aroma of butter cookies fresh from the oven.

As he grabbed one in each hand, his mother, Terese, gave him a quick hug and steered him toward the living room. "Your father and I want to talk to you," she said. "Let's sit down."

Oskar was already seated in his favorite chair, but for once, he wasn't leaning back reading the newspaper. He was sitting forward, his hands clasped in front of him. Terese and Karl settled on the couch.

Haltingly, they explained that a French man, Georges Loigner, had visited them several months earlier. He was looking for children whose parents had been arrested or deported, and the family had come on his radar when Oskar had been sent to Dachau. They explained to Karl that war was in the air, so heavy you could almost taste it, and life for Jews was becoming increasingly dangerous. They recalled Kristallnacht, the loss of the jewelry store, and the increased harassment Karl was enduring at school. Jews who wanted to leave Germany were finding it increasingly hard to find a country that would accept them. They couldn't leave as a family, they explained, but Loigner had paid a considerable sum of money to the Nazis for the papers and exit visas for permission to remove one hundred and twenty-three children from Germany and Austria to take them to France where they would go to school and escape the coming terror.

They told him that above all they wanted him to be safe, and that was no longer possible in Germany. Karl listened intently. He knew others – a few friends even – who had already left. That his family would leave too wasn't shocking, but he hadn't expected to leave alone.

"When?" he asked.

"Tomorrow. You should go to your room and pack."

Dinner that night was a somber affair, despite their best attempts to talk about everyday things. Mostly, I imagine Karl's parents would have focussed on telling him how wonderful it was that he was getting a chance to go to France. He'd learn a new language and see new sights. And they would write letters back and forth until they were reunited – and that would surely be very soon.

At thirteen, Karl was likely scared, but even more probably, feeling a certain frisson of excitement. He was going on an adventure, and, as a bonus, leaving behind the boys who had been bullying him and occasionally throwing rocks and even beating him once or twice.

Before bed, Karl packed his leather suitcase with spare clothes and underwear, his toothbrush, and a favorite book. He looked around his room at everything he was leaving behind. If only he could pack his old featherbed – the one he'd been sleeping under since he was five. He closed the suitcase, reminding himself he was going to have an adventure.

While Karl slept fitfully that night, Terese and Oskar probably lay awake, talking in whispers, or silently gazing at the ceiling. Karl was their only child. Would he be safe? Were they doing the right thing? Would they be able to leave the country and reunite with their son? And when? Already, Terese felt a wound opening up in her chest.

The next morning, they had an early breakfast. Knowing they would soon say goodbye to each other, they must have searched for the important words that needed to be said. But what were those words? And if they found them, would they matter?

They opened the door of the apartment building slowly, careful to be quiet. The morning mist dampened all sounds, even muffling the echo of their footsteps on rain-wet streets as they walked to the Ludwigshafen Hauptbahnhof. The big square building loomed out of the fog. Once inside, they entered a world of chaos and cacophony. Georges Loigner was somewhere in the crowd, counting off one hundred and twenty-three children as their parents hugged them, held them, and shouted last-minute instructions into their ears. Men in uniforms elbowed their way through the throng. Other passengers glanced curiously at the motley group of kids as they made their way to trains belching out steam on the row of tracks.

There was a sense all over Germany, and probably most particularly in train stations across the country, that war was imminent. People were on the move – to go home, to leave home, or perhaps to find an elusive safe haven.

"Alle einsteigen!" The conductor's shout echoed down the platform.

It was time to say goodbye.

Terese hugged her son close to her heart. She didn't want him to have a last image of her with tears running down her face, so she tried to be brave, but her eyes were damp. She wiped at them ferociously. Oskar clasped his son's hand. They watched him board the train to Paris. Would they ever see him again? Would they be able to escape from Germany?

And then Karl was on the train, finding a place to sit and stow his suitcase, listening to the babble of voices from the children, many as young as seven or eight, crying for their parents.

With one connection to another train, the journey took about four hours. Sitting in his compartment were two boys Karl's age, Helmuth Wolff and Hans Rosenberg, who became his first friends in this new reality.

The train pulled into the Gare de L'Est in Paris in the early afternoon. If not for his new friends, Karl would have felt lost in that huge space with signs he couldn't read and a rush of voices speaking a language he didn't understand. As in Germany, and probably everywhere in Europe, people were rushing everywhere, in a hurry to get somewhere – to escape something they knew was coming – but when? And what was it they were running from?

Georges Loigner herded the children onto buses that took them to the Rothchild Hospital, which had enough beds to house them all. A few days later, they moved to their more permanent home at the Chateau de La Guette, situated in the countryside forty kilometers from Paris. The Château dates to the twelfth century. After the Rothschild family purchased it, they offered it as a safe haven for Jewish refugee children.

The children were assigned to their quarters, probably four to a room with bathrooms down the hall. For Karl, the reality of his new life was setting in, and it was no longer an adventure. He missed his parents desperately. My father told me that he used to cry himself to sleep at night, longing for home and the warmth of his mother's arms. But Karl was resilient. I believe it took no more than a couple of weeks for him to adjust and make the best of his situation. I also suspect that as his tears dried, he may have experienced a turmoil of emotions, including anger at having been sent away, even though he knew it was the best decision his parents could have made.

The ten volunteers and teachers at La Guette were acutely aware of the sadness the children carried with them and treated them well. One of those teachers was Flora Loigner, Georges Loigner's wife. Their meals were good, and so was the quality of the education. Letters from his parents were Karl's lifeline. I suspect a few of them were dampened by his tears. I also suspect he collected them in a shoebox under his bed, although, sadly, none of them survived.

The kids followed a fairly strict routine, which also helped settle them in. Mornings were devoted to French lessons to have them speak it well enough that the Germans would believe they were French citizens. They also studied all the traditional subjects like history, science, and math. After lunch, from two to five p.m., they were outside doing physical exercise or indoors taking part in life skills training. They learned how to cook, sew, clean, and take care of themselves. Essentially, these were survival skills. It was no secret war was coming and there were no guarantees where the children would have to eventually go.

One of Loigner's goals was to get the kids into good physical shape, again with an eye to survival. Having heard the stories that had come across the German border during the previous years, many people, including Loigner, knew that many of the children would have to fight to stay alive.

Karl was a good student, quickly becoming proficient in French, but in order to "pass" as a Frenchman he also needed a new name and became Charles, which was a lot less German than Karl. Then only eight months after arriving in La Guette, and one month after war was declared, Charles was uprooted again and sent to Institution Bel-Air, a boarding school in Clémont. More refugee children had arrived and to make room for them, those who spoke French best were moved to make room for the newcomers. Although Charles felt uprooted again, he also took some pride in his language skills. He was ready for his next chapter.

Chapter 2

WAR CLOUDS

While Karl was at La Guette, one of his parents' letters let him know they had escaped from Germany and arrived safely in England. It must have been a relief to all of them to be relatively safe and secure. But for Terese and Oskar, the loss of their country, their livelihood, and their history must have been painful.

For me, Karl's, story begins in 1924 in Ludwigshafen when the young, handsome Carl Sidlin, Charles' biological father, caught Terese's eye. After a year of dating and seeing each other almost every day, Carl proposed and then jumped through a few hoops of tradition before they could marry. He was from Latvia, and, according to Jewish custom and tradition, his Rabbi there had to certify him and his family. Then, according to German law, he had to run an ad in the local newspapers in Saarbrucken, Terese's hometown, and in Ludwigshafen, announcing his intention to marry her. Hearing no objections, and after getting approval from his Rabbi, Carl and Terese were married on March 17, 1925.

Carl had always been drawn to Germany, even though he'd been offered Russian citizenship. He immigrated on November 15, 1908, moving to Ludwigshafen on April 15, 1920, where he apprenticed with Carl Chormann, a watchmaker and goldsmith. When Chormann wanted to retire, Carl offered to buy the business, and in 1921, became the new owner, moving into an apartment directly across the street.

Carl did well, expanding the business to include jewelry sales as well as making watches. He also bought an apartment building in

Gruenerstrasse as an investment, renting out the four apartments. He was well able to provide for his new wife and for the son who was born soon after on January 4, 1926. They named him Severin, simply because they both liked the name.

Life couldn't possibly get any better: they were young and in love and had a precious baby they both doted on.

On January 11, 1926, a Monday morning seven days after the birth of his son, Carl was working in his shop when Herr Weise, an ex-employee, entered, asking to speak to him. They had a pleasant conversation during which Weiss asked if he could come back to work.

"Yes, that would be fine," Carl said. "You can start next Monday."

Weise nodded, put his hand in his pocket, and pulled out a gun. Before Carl had time to register that or even to think, Weise pulled the trigger, putting a bullet through Carl's heart. He died instantly. Weise then turned the gun on two employees, hitting the salesperson, Fraulein Lemke, in the right lower leg, and Herr Hinlan, a watchmaker who'd had time to dash behind a cupboard, in the left hip, just grazing the skin. Then Weise turned the gun on himself, pointed it at his right temple, and pulled the trigger.

Was it a hate crime? My detailed investigation tells me it was not. The newspaper reporting on the incident and the subsequent police investigation, stated, "The content of various cards that Weise left behind, suggest the offender was insane." At Carl's funeral, crowds of people followed the casket, paying their respects to a well-loved friend and neighbor.

I can't imagine the grief that engulfed Terese. Her entire life had been torn apart by one, crazy, mad act of insanity. This was only the first time her life would be disrupted and torn apart. However, for the sake of her baby, she had to carry on. She did not have the luxury of taking to her bed and wailing at the gods. She inherited the apartment building at Gruenerstrasse 1 as well as the watchmaker's shop. Because she now had to support herself and her baby, she hired a nanny and set about learning the business. With the kindness and help of the employees, the business continued to do well and even began to grow.

She marketed directly to the employees at IG Farben (now BASF) developing a reputation for excellence and integrity. She owed a lot of her new business to referrals from satisfied customers. She extended credit to almost anyone, and people would stop in periodically to make a payment on their account. She based her transactions on trust and had very few delinquent accounts.

A Jewish tradition with roots in the Old Testament, says, "If you remember a name, then you will remember the person." And so, traditionally, children are named after deceased relatives in order to honor them. To remember her husband and pay him tribute, Terese changed her son's name to Karl. The legal change was registered on September 23, 1926, eight months after his birth.

Terese's new routine involved going to work every day at the shop while the nanny looked after Karl. She had no social life, and that was fine with her – but not with her brothers, Eugene and Leopold, who wanted her to marry again. Leopold wanted to introduce her to a friend, Abraham Herschel Oskar Schwarz, known as Oskar, who lived in Berlin. Because Oskar had experience as a watchmaker, Leopold thought it would be a good match.

Oskar was born in 1891 in Przemysl, which is now in eastern Poland, about six miles from the Ukrainian border. After enough prodding and pushing, and Leopold promising that Oskar would help run the business and adopt Karl, Terese finally agreed to meet him. They married on November 12, 1929. To my mind, it has all the earmarks of an arranged marriage, but the longevity of their relationship through some hard times, tells me that whatever the initial motivation, it worked out for both of them.

1929 was also the year Germany's fortunes began to crumble. While Germany had been recovering nicely from World War I and Ludwigshafen was growing as an industrial center, the United States entered the Great Depression in October of that year. America had loaned Germany a great deal of money after World War I to rebuild their country, but when the Depression hit, the United States needed and demanded repayment of the loans. Germany didn't have the money to comply, so they started printing currency indiscriminately. This began a chain reaction that led to hyperinflation by the early 1930s.

At one point, the German Reichsmark was trading at one billion to one U.S. dollar. Prices skyrocketed out of control, companies shut down, and people lost jobs. Unemployment was rampant.

In the early 1930s, when Hitler walked onto the political stage and said he would restore employment by rebuilding the German military and giving everyone a job, he found a ready audience. He also singled out the Jews. "The reason you don't have anything is because they have it all." In a healthy economy, his words would probably not have resonated, but conditions were so bad in Germany that people eagerly accepted the idea of a scapegoat. They linked the Depression to Germany's humiliating defeat in World War I, believing the current government was weak and couldn't solve the desperate economic crisis. As a result, the Nazi party which won only 2.6 percent of the national vote in the 1928 election, won 18.3 percent in the 1930 election and 37.3 percent in 1932, making the Nazis the largest political party in Germany.

Hitler became Chancellor of Germany in January 1933. He came to power legitimately. There was no government takeover, no coup d'état, and no military takeover. Everything he did was legal.

Meanwhile, Terese and Oskar worked side by side in the jewelry store while Karl's nanny, who he had come to adore, continued to look after him. He was almost four when he started attending nursery school, and shortly after that, on September 4, 1931, Oskar adopted him, changing his name officially, to Karl Schwarz, and he was no longer a Sidlin!

At age five, Karl entered Kindergarten, and a year later, public school. His childhood was as normal as it could have been, given the upheaval of the society around him. He was probably largely unaware of the changes that affected Jews, but I believe he must have felt some of them. Possibly some children were not allowed to play with him. Even before Hitler assumed power, when one of Terese's friends wanted to enroll her child in Karl's nursery school, she was turned down with the explanation from the director, "I can't take any more Jewish children because I'm afraid the non-Jews will remove their kids from the school."

Hitler consolidated his power quickly and in three months abolished the German constitution. The German people, living in a sovereign, democratic nation, simply and willingly gave up their rights.

The Nazis started issuing decrees affecting Jewish life in Germany, notably and firstly, the Nuremberg Laws in September 1935, because they wanted to put their ideas about race into law. They believed in the false theory that the world is divided into distinct races that are not equally strong and valuable. The Nazis considered Germans to be members of the supposedly superior "Aryan" race and saw it as the strongest, and most valuable race of all. According to the Nazis, Jews were not Aryans and belonged to a separate race that was inferior to all other races. The Nazis believed that the presence of Jews in Germany threatened the German people, and they had to separate Jews from other Germans to protect and strengthen the country.

The Nuremberg Laws removed German citizenship from Jews. Even if they were born and raised in Germany, they were no longer German citizens. They were now stateless. Imagine having your identity ripped from you with one stroke of the pen. I often wonder how my grandparents felt. Anger? Despair? Disbelief? There may not be a word to accurately describe that sense of helplessness and loss of identity.

Some other restrictions of the Nuremberg laws included a ban on inter-marrying of Jews and Germans; Jews were no longer admitted to municipal hospitals; Jewish businesses had to paint a yellow star of David on their shop windows; German courts could no longer cite legal opinions written by Jewish legal scholars; Jews were not allowed to be officers in the German army; non-Jewish women were not allowed to work as household help in Jewish homes. As a result of the latter, Terese had to let Karl's nanny go, breaking both their hearts as they hugged and said tear-filled goodbyes.

The Nuremberg Laws changed everything. On January 10, 1938, Terese had to sell her apartment building on Gruenerstrasse 1 to Franz Hage, a brewmaster, because the Nazis had been putting pressure on her daily for some time, telling her if she didn't sell, they would confiscate it. She sold it at about fifty percent of market value.

Oskar and Terese could no longer take Karl to the park because the park benches had signs: "No Jews allowed." They couldn't travel because hotels had signs: "No dogs and no Jews." Some children at school would no longer play with Karl, and he began to hear the words, "Judenschwein."

Perhaps one of the most painful new laws, not part of the Nuremberg Laws, was the name change decree, called the Law on Alteration of Family and Personal Names, that went into effect in the middle of 1938. Every Jewish man had to legally change his name to add the word Israel and women had to add Sarah. Oskar became Oskar Israel Schwarz and Terese became Terese Sarah Schwarz. The Nazis changed every marriage and birth certificate to comply with the new law. One purpose of the law was to easily identify Jews, but that was the simplest explanation. The real one goes far deeper. Names are extremely important in the Jewish faith and culture. It states in the

Old Testament 1 Chronicles 1-9, "I Am Not Forgotten - He Knows My Name!"

And so, Jewish people name their babies after dead relatives to honor them. The Nazis knew what they were doing. They were thrusting a dagger into five thousand years of Jewish tradition and culture, all part of the process of marginalizing them.

On November 9, 1938, Oskar, Terese, and Karl lived through Kristallnacht, a night so infamous, that some historians have called it "The beginning of the final solution of the Holocaust."

Kristallnacht means the "night of broken glass" and is a name that comes from the shards of broken glass that littered the streets after the windows of Jewish-owned stores, buildings, homes, and synagogues were smashed. The pogrom was carried out by the Nazi Party's Sturmabteilung (SA) and Schutzstaffel (SS) paramilitary along with some Hitler Youth and civilians, although many paramilitary traded in their uniforms for civilian clothes to give the impression of a popular citizen's uprising, supposedly set off by the assassination of the German diplomat Ernst von Rath by Herschel Grynszpan, a seventeen-year-old German-born Polish Jew living in Paris.

Jewish homes, hospitals, and schools were ransacked by attackers wielding sledgehammers. Rioters destroyed 267 synagogues throughout Germany, Austria, and the Sudetenland in German-occupied Czechoslovakia. Over seven thousand Jewish businesses were damaged or destroyed. They broke down the doors of apartments and houses, trashed the furniture, and destroyed people's personal effects. They destroyed all the Jewish cemeteries, repurposing the gravestones for cobblestones to pave the streets erasing again centuries of Jewish history and culture. Many Jews were beaten up, hundreds died, and about thirty thousand were arrested and sent to concentration camps.

Kristallnacht marked the first time that the Nazis arrested Jews en masse simply because they were Jews. British historian, Martin

Gilbert wrote that no event in the history of German Jews between 1933 and 1945 was so widely reported as it was taking place. On November 11, 1938, the Times of London reported, "No foreign propagandist bent upon blackening Germany before the world, could outdo the tale of burnings and beatings, of blackguardly assaults of defenseless and innocent people, which disgraced that country yesterday."

The Schwarzes huddled in their apartment when the riots began. They'd had no warning and no prescient knowledge that their lives would be on the line on this ordinary night. Their ears were filled with the sounds of hateful shouts, terrified screams, and shattering glass. They wondered if their jewelry store would survive? Would the mob come to their door?

Then it came – the pounding of a fist. "Mach auf!" Taking a deep breath, Oskar told his wife and son to stay still. He opened the door. Two uniformed men holding rifles grabbed him by the arms. "You're under arrest."

Oskar knew better than to ask why. With no chance to give Terese even a backward glance, he was marched out the door, down the stairs, and into a waiting vehicle. One image registered in his mind as he ducked his head to get in: the jewelry store across the street was unharmed.

How had it survived? The riot had been well-organized with specific orders of what should and should not be destroyed. Oskar's store was to be spared because it contained gold and jewels the government did not want to be endangered by looters. They believed that the merchandise was state property, and the state had other plans for it.

Oskar was sent to Dachau just outside Munich. It wasn't yet the notorious concentration camp it became in the 1940s. At the time it served as a prison for dissenters, homosexuals, Jews, Communists, and political opponents.

Terese and Karl had no idea where Oskar was. After a sleepless night of fighting down their panic, they greeted the day with a mixture of relief that they and their shop across the street had survived and fear for Oskar. Was he alive? And if he was, where had they taken him? Terese feared the most unimaginable: that he was gone – shot, just like her beloved Carl.

Keeping a firm grip on her terror, she hurried to the Gestapo office several blocks away. The officer she talked to was surprisingly cordial, even apologizing that he had no information about her husband. No news. I suspect she must have briefly felt some relief that she hadn't been given the worst news she could imagine. But she had to know where he was.

She went back the next day and the next. Where was he? Where was her husband? Karl was in a daze. Not knowing what else to do, he went to school. When the bullying escalated, his teachers simply looked away. Were they ashamed or afraid or did they simply not care?

Finally, Terese got the news: Oskar was at Dachau. He was alive!

He was registered into Dachau on November 12, 1938, and released six weeks later on December 20. Many have speculated that Jewish prisoners got released from Dachau only after agreeing to turn over their businesses to the Nazis. I don't know if that was the case for Oskar, but in February 1939, Oskar got a letter from the mayor's office in Ludwigshafen with the subject line, "Elimination of Jews from German Economic Life." It went on to say that: "Due to the existing conditions in the watch, gold, and silverware trade business, Jewish businesses of this kind must be categorically dissolved. For the dissolution of such enterprises, it's necessary, however, to not allow re-openings of such stores in its place in the foreseeable future."

Certainly, it was to the advantage of the authorities that the store had not been damaged on Kristallnacht. That doesn't appear to have been a coincidence. I doubt the letter came to Oskar as a surprise. He probably would have been far more surprised if he had been allowed to keep operating his shop. He probably had already begun hiding some inventory and possibly some of his earnings. He had already applied for an exit visa, and they were expensive.

As my father said many years later when I asked him about his parents' escape, "They bribed their way out."

The Nazis ordered Oskar to do a complete inventory of the business, which he valued at 7,500 Reichsmarks, possibly about $15,000 USD. The Nazis then brought in their appraiser, Richard Albrecht, who estimated the value at 6,000 Reichsmarks.

But Oskar also looked for and found a buyer for the business, Herr Karl Schenk. The Nazis approved the sale of the business for 6,000 Reichsmarks and gave Schenk an exemption under the Law for the Protection of Retailers that no competitive business could open in the neighborhood for a period of two years. The sales agreement between Oskar and Schenk stated that the proceeds from the sale of the business were to be paid into a blocked account at the State Bank of Germany. This meant that Karl Schenk paid the agreed-upon price, but Oskar never received it because the account was blocked from him. In other words, the Nazis stole the money, as was typical for businesses that were seized from Jews.

Again, I don't think Oskar was shocked. I wouldn't be surprised if he and Terese had begun sewing valuables and money into the linings of their coats and jackets.

In May 1939, two months after sending their son to safety in France, Oskar and Terese finally received their exit visas. Taking what they could – and it wasn't a lot – they crossed the channel to England. They no longer owned a shop or a thriving business. They were refugees.

Chapter 3

IN FRANCE

Charles felt a wave of relief wash over him when he got the letter from his mother: "We're in England. We're safe!"

Her letters were his only remaining ties to home. The place he had grown up no longer existed for him. No matter how much he longed for those familiar streets or the comfort of his room, surrounded by the familiar bits and pieces he had grown up with, none of that existed anymore.

He had only his mother's letters and his daily routine of school and sports at the Institution Bel-Air in Clémont. The routine probably helped settle him and make him feel like these unconventional times were close to normal.

Then, in May 1940, Germany invaded France, and Charles' world was upended again. The Nazi army rolled in largely unimpeded, taking over the northern part of the country as well as the strip of land down the Atlantic coast. The southern part of France was now ruled by the Vichy government headed by Marshal Philippe Pétain. It wasn't necessarily a free France because many French citizens collaborated with the Germans, but it was not yet officially under German control.

Charles experienced the German soldiers as an almost benign force, walking around as though France was theirs, the war was over, and they had won. After effortlessly taking over Poland and being welcomed in Austria, the soldiers could be forgiven for thinking that this war was a simple walk in the park. If Charles encountered one, they would nod to each other, say "Bonjour," and walk on.

However, the director of the school wasn't convinced that his children would be safe for long. Many Parisians felt the same way. Thousands gathered daily at the train stations in a chaotic bid to go south. The director of the Institution Bel-Air decided to take all the kids to his estate in Poitiers, still in occupied France, but farther from Paris and therefore, safer.

On June 11, 1940, the kids arrived at Gare Montparnasse to a scene of utter bedlam, far too reminiscent of Charles' hasty departure from the Ludwigshafen Hauptbahnhof. But this scene of chaos was even worse. The school director ushered them through the crowds, the heaps of baggage, struggling porters, and frantic parents searching for lost children. An odor of panic hung in the air as strong as the smell of unwashed bodies.

Somehow, the director managed to squeeze the kids onto the train. There was nowhere to sit, The compartments were stuffed, the corridors overflowing with people and their baggage. Women were crying, babies wailing, and children shouting out to each other – the air so thick it was almost impossible to breathe.

The journey that should have taken four hours went on interminably. By the time they got off the train in Poitiers and the kids tumbled onto the platform, they were gasping and exhausted.

Charles felt utterly disoriented, displaced yet again, but like the other children, he carved out a small space for himself, and tried, once again, to live a normal life.

Impossible. For reasons known only to them, the Germans were flying missions in the area, often across the surrounding fields, strafing the ground, and aiming for anyone who happened to be outside. The children were too terrified to set foot outdoors. Even on sunny days, they stayed inside.

After only three months, the school director had had enough. Poitiers was no better than Paris. It was still in the occupied zone and the German Luftwaffe was making the place untenable. On September 23, 1940, he took the children back to Clémont. In the meantime, La Guette had closed and Loigner had to disperse all the children, including those staying at Clémont, to fourteen separate facilities.

On January 1, 1941, Charles was sent to the Hotel des Anglais in La Bourboule in the unoccupied portion of France. The hotel was a big square brick building with sloping roofs in a pretty town set in a small green valley, a holiday place in better times. It was safer for the children, but all of Europe including Great Britain, Canada, and Australia were now fully engaged against the German-Italian Axis, and an icy cold winter had set in. By now, Charles was probably no longer feeling fully displaced every time he had to move. He was resigned to the fact that this was now his life. Would it ever be different? Would he ever know stability again? He focused on two things: letters from his mother, and simply staying alive, warm and fed – and that was no easy task.

There wasn't enough coal to heat the rooms where they slept, and there was rarely enough food to feed hunger pangs, especially not those of a fifteen-year-old boy. All the children were constantly hungry. Food was rationed and many food items including most vegetables, simply weren't available. Many children, including Charles, were also growing out of their clothes, but if their ankles and wrists were exposed or moth holes could no longer be repatched, there was no use complaining. New sweaters and trousers were luxury items beyond their reach.

One of Charles' bunkmates went out into the fields one evening, broke into a barn, and stole a 50 kg (110 pounds) bag of oats meant for feeding the horses. He brought it back and dragged it up to their room. Charles rammed handfuls of the dry oats into a shoebox, crammed the lid on, and hid it under his bed, stuffing handfuls into his mouth whenever his stomach contracted painfully in hunger.

All the children were assigned chores. Charles, my father, who I remember as having trouble boiling an egg, was assigned to work in the kitchen as a cook. He recalled clearly how he was not allowed to peel potatoes with a potato peeler, because it might remove some of the flesh along with the peel – and every tiny bit of potato flesh was precious.

On July 6, 1941, seven months after arriving in La Bourboule, Charles was sent to Dieulfit to the École de Beauvallon and then, in October of that year, to the École Hoteliere Amedee Gasquet in Clermont-Ferrand. In January 1942, he returned to La Bourboule to a new facility, Ville Marguerite. During his three-and-a-half years in France, he moved eight times. Sometimes, he was lucky enough to be with Helmuth and Hans, the friends he made when he first arrived in France. Often the three boys were separated.

Were the multiple moves deliberate? I believe they were. A moving target is harder to hit. We can never be certain that traveling from place to place was a major factor in keeping him safe, but I do believe it helped.

By the end of 1942, Germany occupied all of France. If you were a Jew, your life was in danger. A year and a half earlier, in May 1941, the French had started rounding up Jews and arresting them. If you were walking down the street or riding your bicycle, you'd be stopped and asked for your papers. If you were Jewish, you'd be arrested and sent to Drancy or Pithiviers, transit camps where Jews were aggregated before being deported to Auschwitz. The deportations started in March 1942, and approximately 1,000 people were transported each month to Auschwitz.

After his last move to Ville Marguerite, Charles was essentially in hiding, knowing that every stranger who knocked on the door and every face he met in the street when he dared to go out, could arrest him and send him away, condemning him to certain death. Confined to the villa, he teetered on the edge of boredom and terror.

Georges Loigner was well aware that France was no longer a safe haven for his kids, and it was certainly foolhardy to keep a large group together in one place. How soon would locals become suspicious? And who were the informers? Undoubtedly they existed. To get them out of France, he enlisted the help of an organization he worked with, the Oeuvre de Secours aux Enfants (OSE), or Children's Welfare Organization, a Jewish charity that ran fourteen children's homes in Vichy France, and played a key role in rescuing Jewish children in France during World War II.

OSE was unique among children's aid agencies because while they did their utmost to save the children, they also worked covertly with the French Resistance. Like the OSE, Loigner also worked both overtly and covertly.

While Charles restlessly paced the halls of Ville Marguerite or worked in the kitchen, Loigner was planning to move him and the other children to Switzerland. None of the kids knew. To tell them at these early stages could have spelled disaster. I'm sure Loigner and others involved in the strategizing would have wanted to tell the kids it was going to be okay. They saw how worried and scared they were. They heard the younger ones crying at night as they tried to flee into sleep, but their safety demanded the utmost secrecy.

Then Charles stopped receiving letters from his mother. He thought, maybe they got lost. They'd pick up again soon. But one week went by and then another, and then it was two months and three, and Charles began to worry. What had happened? Had his parents been killed in a bombing raid? Had they died some other way? Or maybe the British had finally decided to incarcerate them. He tried to tamp down his anxiety. The worst of it was that they were probably far more worried about him than he was about them, and he had no way of reaching them. Maybe he should just be fatalistic. This was war and yes, the worst things happened and you never knew when it would be you or someone you loved.

If Charles was feeling anxious, his mother was probably near panic. While they were relatively safe in England, her son was in the thick of the war. Was he injured or possibly dead? Or had he been sent to one of the "camps" they'd been hearing about? She could imagine nothing worse.

Six months passed before Charles finally had another letter, and wrote back to tell his parents all was well. Why the gap? He never knew. The only explanation was the one that explained everything else – there was a war.

On October 3, 1942, the director, or possibly an assistant, or even Loigner himself, told Charles and three other boys, including Helmuth and Hans, to gather together some bare necessities and prepare to leave. Those items didn't include the letters Charles' mother had sent. How hard it must have been to leave behind that link that mattered so much. They headed to the train station again, this time traveling to Annemasse, a town in the Haute-Savoie on the Swiss border and only seven miles from Geneva. Annemasse was also, not surprisingly given its location, a center for the French Resistance.

The boys weren't told that their ultimate destination was Switzerland. They didn't have proper exit visas from France nor permission to enter Switzerland. If they were questioned by the authorities, they didn't want to be able to give anything up. But because they were headed to Annemasse on the border with Switzerland, they probably figured it out all on their own. I'm unsure how many kids were on that train. It may have been just Charles and his friends, and they may very well have been traveling alone.

The train ride would have been exciting, frightening, and harrowing for the boys. German soldiers and French collaborators walked up and down the aisles, checking papers. Would their forged papers pass the test? Was their French good enough that the Germans would believe they were French youths going to a new home?

In an interview recorded years later, Loigner mentioned multiple trips, once taking fifty young children who started wandering from car to car to amuse themselves on the long train ride. With so many to look after, Loigner didn't notice at first that a handful were missing. After a quick search, he found them in a wagon where some elderly German passengers were smiling at them and feeding them candy and chocolates.

"Who are these lovely children," they asked.

He told them his well-prepared story. They were from the area around Marseille where their homes in the old port had been destroyed. They had been ill and were being sent to a center where they would go to school and also regain their health. Loigner believed the Germans felt great compassion for them, because they brought them back to the kids' wagon, even handing out more treats. In Loigner's own words, "Not all Germans were bad."

On their journey, Charles and his friends relaxed after the Germans gave their papers a cursory glance and handed them back, but their anxiety grew again as they pulled into the Annemasse train station. Once again, to leave the station, they had to show their papers, praying they would pass. For Charles and the other older children, an added concern was not to show they were worried. They had to act casual, to breathe normally, and to hide their trembling hands.

Georges Loigner, who was very active in the French Resistance at this time, met them at the station and took them to a safe house where they stayed only a few days. On October 7 at 2 a.m., Loigner shook the four boys awake. It was time to go.

Charles and his friends were instantly alert. This was it!

They had no time to feel anticipatory, afraid, or even excited. All the emotions they'd ever felt had rolled themselves into a big, heavy ball that lodged in their chests. They were focused on only one thing: go to the border and follow Loigner's instructions. After that, whatever happened was up to the fates or God or their own luck.

Loigner drove them to the Swiss border. He wasn't particularly concerned about patrols because the Italians were guarding the Franco-Swiss border and were fairly kind, usually closing their eyes or looking the other way when people crossed.

He led them to a short barbed wire fence. "You climb over here," he said, "and then you walk in that direction," pointing out the direction to Geneva.

Did they hug him goodbye? Were there tears? Or were they too focused? I suspect there was a mix of emotions, including intense gratitude for everything Loigner had done for them. The boys climbed over the fence, and soon after, took off their shoes and socks to wade across the Arve River. When they climbed up the far bank, they were in Switzerland.

They took a minute to sit in the damp grass and put their shoes and socks back on before walking across the fields in the direction of Geneva. A wave of relief washed over them, followed almost immediately by elation. They had done it! They had escaped! They were free!

They wanted to run, dance, and skip. It wasn't a dream. They were actually free! But they had been walking less than an hour when a Swiss border guard approached them. He was used to picking up refugees crossing from Annemasse and taking them to the border patrol station where the captain grilled them. Of all the questions he asked, the most important was, "How old are you?"

Charles and two of his friends were sixteen. The other boy was fifteen. The captain explained that Switzerland had an age cut-off of fifteen years for child refugees. The younger boy could stay. The others would be escorted back to the French border.

Where Charles and his friends had just reached the heights of elation only an hour before, they now sank into a pit of despair. After everything they had been through, they had to go back? It had all been futile? Charles couldn't grasp it. It had to be a horrible dream. He was here – safe – in Switzerland. His feet were firmly rooted on Swiss soil. And he had to leave? Much as he tried to believe the captain was making a mistake, he knew from the frown on his face, and the sad eyes of the border guard, it was true. He was going back. And this time, not to a safe house. He and his friends had no money and no door to knock on to ask for shelter.

They would inevitably be captured by the Nazis and sent to Auschwitz. All of this flashed through his mind in an instant. His dread grew to a size he didn't think his body could contain. And yet, he couldn't allow himself to cry. If not for himself, he had to be brave for his friends. If he broke down, then all hope was truly lost.

They followed the border guard out of the captain's office and back to the field they had so recently crossed. But now they were walking in the wrong direction – not toward freedom, but to captivity and probably worse. When they arrived back at the border, the guard stopped. "Here you are," he said, pointing straight ahead. "There's France, and you have to go back." He turned and pointed in the other direction. "Geneva is that way. I have to do the rest of my rounds."

With that, he turned his back on them and walked away.

Chapter 4

ANOTHER ESCAPE

The boys watched the Swiss guard walk away, their hearts beating so hard, that they swore they could be heard a mile away. Was it true? Were they free to go? Were they in a dream or still a nightmare? They waited until he had disappeared from sight before turning to each other with sighs of relief, their grins wide and then wider when they realized they would make it after all. But they were cautious. They could cover the four miles to Geneva in an hour if they walked on the road, but they couldn't take a chance on another patrol, so they angled off across a field and then started climbing the slopes of the mountain, dew-wet grasses and underbrush soaking through their pants and patches of snow waterlogging their feet through their shoes. Gusts of wind scattering wet snow flurries chilled them to the bone.

But the closer they got, the more their excitement grew. No one was walking on this slope where there was no trail, just low-growing trees and scrub with prickly burrs to stick to their pants and socks. They were invisible from the road. Safe.

In his pocket, Charles carried a precious piece of paper Georges Loigner had handed him before he'd left them at the border: the address of a church where the pastor was known to help refugee children sent his way. When they reached Geneva, they ducked down side streets or tried to blend in with the crowds hurrying to work. Following the sketchy directions Loigner had given them, they arrived at the old stone church and found the small rectory around the corner. They banged on the scarred wooden door. The Pastor quickly opened it and pulled the boys inside.

They were hit by a rush of warmth – heat they hadn't felt in years that radiated straight into their numbed fingers and toes. The pastor showed them where to hang their wet jackets and brought them into the kitchen where he indicated they should sit at a long wooden table while he prepared breakfast. To Charles and his friends, it must have looked like a feast. They'd been living on watery soup, rough bread, thin porridge, and horse meal for so long, that they had almost forgotten what an abundance of food looked or smelled like. The pastor presented them with a long baguette, boiled eggs, sausages, bacon, hunks of rich farm cheese, coffee, cream, and butter – imagine – butter!

The boys tried to remember their manners, but one taste of such extravagance and all they could do was eat as fast and as much as their stomachs could hold. I doubt the pastor would have minded. He'd seen enough hunger in the past years to understand that for these children, arriving in Switzerland was like landing on a different planet.

With breakfast finished, and feeling better than they had in months, the boys told the pastor their story, including their crossing into Switzerland from France and being apprehended by the border guard and sent back.

When they were finished, the pastor explained that the child refugee program in Switzerland was administered by the Swiss National Police. He gave them directions to the police station and gave them money to take the tram with the instructions, "Tell them who you are – that you are German-Jewish refugees who were hiding in France and came into Switzerland – and you're fifteen years old, born in 1927."

Charles and his friends followed the pastor's instructions, hopping onto the crowded tram, wondering, would it work? Would the police believe them? Did they look too old to be only fifteen? Leaving the warmth of the pastor's house, the chill of anxiety descended again. But they were processed at the station without incident and sent to a refugee camp the government had set up in the Stade de Varade, a popular sports stadium. There, they were reunited with the younger friend they had left behind at the border. You can imagine his joy at knowing his friends had escaped the terrible fate of going back to France. The accommodations at the arena were adequate, only meant to be temporary until more permanent placements could be found. The five hundred or so children were supplied with a cot and given a mess kit for their meals and a canteen for water.

Charles stayed about a week, during which time he probably got more news than he'd had for a while. Information about what was happening to German Jews during this time filtered down to the general public – certainly not the full horrors, but it was no secret they were being rounded up and shipped to transit camps, and then on to concentration camps. In Eastern Europe, Jews were herded together and enclosed in ghettoes. Charles would not have heard the details that between November 1941 and late October 1942, just as he made good his escape to Switzerland, German authorities had confined more than fifty thousand Jews in ghettos just in the Baltic states alone.

They spared a small minority for exploitation as forced laborers, interning them in special German sections of the Baltic and Belorussian ghettos, segregated from those few local Jews whose survival the SS and police had permitted, generally to exploit special occupational skills.

In the vast network of forced labor camps, prisoners were compelled to work in construction, agriculture, or manufacturing to support the war effort. By the end of the war, more than 14 million people had been exploited in these camps.

The Nazis had set up an intricate variety of camps. Captured allied soldiers, mainly American, French, British, Polish, and Soviets, were sent to prisoner of war (POW) camps. Many women were forced to have sex with German soldiers in sex slave camps.

The death/extermination camps were built with the explicit purpose of murdering Jews. There were six, all located in Poland: Auschwitz-Birkenau, Sobibor, Treblinka, Chelmno, Majdanek, and Belzec. Typically, trains would arrive and the prisoners would disembark. A very small number, the lucky ones, would be selected for work detail. The rest would be sent to the showers, which were actually gas chambers.

Auschwitz.org explains the extermination procedure:

"SS men escorted the men, women, and children selected for death to the gas chambers. Trucks carried those too infirm to walk, and the rest marched. These people had to disrobe before entering the gas chambers.

"The SS men kept the people fated to die unaware of what awaited them. They were told that they were being sent to the camp, but that they first had to undergo disinfection and bathe. After the victims undressed, they were taken into the gas chamber, locked in, and killed with Zyklon B gas.

"After they were killed, Sonderkommando prisoners dragged the corpses out of the gas chambers. They cut off the women's hair and removed all metal dental work and jewelry. Then they burned the corpses in pits, on pyres, or in the crematorium furnaces. (Until September 1942, some of the corpses were buried in mass graves; these corpses were burned from September to November 1942.)

"Bones that did not burn completely were ground to powder with pestles and then dumped, along with the ashes, in the rivers Soła and Vistula and nearby ponds, or strewn in the fields as fertilizer, or used as landfill on uneven ground and in marshes."

Although Charles almost certainly had no knowledge of these horrific camps or the gas chambers, I'm sure he heard enough to fear deeply for any friends he had left behind in Ludwigshafen and to be grateful for the safety Switzerland offered him. He wasn't free to go where he wanted. The Swiss government had created a long list of restrictions on refugees, but he was alive and safe from any risk of deportation.

Still, Switzerland was a tiny island in a sea of German-occupied Europe. How could such a small country continue its independence? The Nazi advance had been inexorable throughout the summer of 1942. It wasn't until late that year in the battle for the city of Stalingrad that the tide began to turn. Stress was the constant background music in Charles' life – and not just for himself. His parents had endured the Blitzkrieg in 1940, a ferocious firestorm bombing on London that didn't end until May 1941. What was next? Surely there was more to come.

Charles' only comfort was his mother's letters that had resumed again, talking almost cheerfully, about their life in London. Oskar still repaired watches, working from his apartment at 50 Compayne Gardens near the Finchley Road underground station in London. If Charles was thankful for his life in Switzerland, he was doubly grateful for his parents' circumstances.

Because the British were concerned about spies, most German refugees in England were incarcerated, even though they were almost all Jewish refugees fleeing for their lives. Terese and Oskar escaped that particular fate. Many others did as well, but I don't know what the reasoning was behind the official decision. Oskar's papers were titled, Male Enemy Alien – Exemption from internment – Refugee.

Chapter 5

SWITZERLAND

After a week at Stade de Varade, Charles was sent to the Hotel Heiden as another temporary measure before putting him to work in more permanent quarters. Ironically, Charles had vacationed there with his parents once, and the beautiful setting on the shores of Lake Constance was dear and familiar to him. At the same time, it felt like those days existed in an entirely different life.

A week after his arrival, the administration for the Home for Refugee Children Waldeck, in Langenbruck, requested Charles' services as a cook. Various facilities and organizations in Switzerland would regularly write letters to the National Police, asking to hire certain children, usually the older ones. They would have had information already that Charles had experience in various kitchens in France. The police would look over the application and if they granted permission, would send Charles to the facility, which would pay him for his services. However, half his pay would be placed in a bank account he could only access with permission from the police.

He also had to agree to the rules and regulations for refugee children. He had to abide by a curfew. He couldn't leave the city without specific written permission from the police. He couldn't congregate in large groups or perform public speeches. He had to agree to leave Switzerland as soon as it was feasible to do so, and lastly "To use at any time and everywhere a discrete and correct attitude that takes into account the position of a refugee enjoying Switzerland's right of residence."

Translation: "Be grateful we're allowing you to stay here."

In early May 1943, he had a new job posting at the Labor Camp for Internees in Arisdorf in the canton of Basel. Two months later, he was back in Langenbruck at the Children's Sanatorium Basel. Between then and September 1945, he moved locations five more times. Occasionally, he was reunited with Hans and Helmuth, but with the frequent moves, he never had time to settle and make other friends. It must have been lonely, but I also think he adopted a stoic, fatalistic approach. The frequent relocations were not his choice. In fact, given his list of restrictions, he had very few decisions he could make for himself. Still, he was healthy and alive, a privilege many others were denied.

In early 1944, his work opportunities changed. He was no longer peeling potatoes or slicing up carrots in the kitchen. Instead, he'd been hired by a Zionist organization, possibly funded by American Jewry. That was fine with the Swiss government, which didn't care where he worked as long as he was employed and not dependent on the state.

His role was to visit with Jewish people who wanted to emigrate to Palestine and help them fill out the necessary paperwork. For Charles, the language barrier presented a challenge. Most of those wishing to go spoke Czech, Polish, Hungarian, and other Eastern European languages. Charles spoke German and French and the papers were also in German or French.

Many years later, while riding on a train between Geneva and Lausanne with my father, I discovered for the first time the full extent of his history there when he said, "This train brings back a lot of memories."

"How so?" I asked.

"During the war, I took his train almost every day."

"Why?"

And so he told me about the work he had done and revealed how he had also become caught up in the idea of living communally on a kibbutz on the land promised to the Jews two thousand years before. It was to be a utopia: people caring about each other, looking after each other, and not worrying about ownership of anything. According to the literature Charles read, the kibbutz operated under the premise that all income generated by it and its members went into a common pool that was used to run it, make investments, and guarantee mutual and reciprocal aid and responsibility between members. Kibbutz members received the same budget, according to family size, regardless of their job or position.

Possibly because Charles had been separated from his parents for so long, and also that he had not had the opportunity to establish intimate relationships, either in France or Switzerland, the idea of a close-knit community must have appealed to him quite strongly. It didn't take long before he began considering the move to Palestine along with all the people he was talking to.

When the war ended in May 1945, Charles' parents expected him to come to them in England. Instead, flooded with visions of an ideal community he could call his own, he boarded the steamship S.S. Lima on September 2, 1945, out of Barcelona bound for Palestine. For him and so many other refugees, it truly was the promised land. He arrived on September 11 and was immediately transported to Kutzoh Ianot, a kibbutz near Ramat David, not too far from Haifa.

Like many other kibbutzim, Kutzoh Ianot grew oranges, and Charles spent most of his days planting, weeding and harvesting the large groves of trees under a hot, dry sun. He grew disenchanted with the kibbutz way of life quickly, saying in later years that he'd been brainwashed and the kibbutz was more communist than Russia. He owned nothing. When his shirt and pants needed laundering, he would turn them in and be handed a fresh set of clothing.

His parents sent a small stack of prepaid postage aerograms so that he could write to them. The kibbutz confiscated them. No one was allowed personal effects – not even airmail letter paper.

He started fighting with himself. While he hated being there, he felt it was his duty to stay and make a difference. After everything the Jews had been through – and he was now hearing the stories firsthand from survivors and relatives of survivors – surely he had to do something to build a place the Jewish people could call home.

But the life there wore him down until he felt that along with not owning personal possessions, he couldn't even own his own thoughts, needs, or desires. This was not the community he'd longed to find.

He finally sent a letter to his parents who sent him the fare to come to England. In 1946, he boarded a steamer in Haifa and sailed to Marseille. From there, he boarded a train for Paris, memories nudging his heart as he changed trains at Gare Montparnasse, quieter now – nothing like the chaotic scene he'd experienced years before when he'd left the city with more than a hundred other children.

From Paris, he took a train to the coast, and then a ferry across the Channel to reunite with his parents in London. Although my father was prone to say "I don't remember" when asked to recall those emotional memories, I think it's easy to conjure up what that meeting must have been like. Terese hadn't seen her son for seven years. He'd been a boy, only thirteen when she'd waved goodbye at a train pulling out of the Ludwigshafen station. Now she was welcoming back a young man of twenty, taller than she was. She had to reach up to wrap her arms around him. She was a soft, gentle, loving woman. I'm sure she must have wept with joy.

I'm certain Charles did too, although he may have tried to hide his tears. Like Charles, Oskar was probably also putting on a stoic front, shaking his hand fervently instead of embracing him.

Charles accompanied his parents back to their apartment and immediately began his English studies, not only because he needed to work, but also because he wanted to fit in. Not surprisingly, anyone speaking German in England at that time was eyed with a great deal of suspicion. But Charles, Terese, and Oskar all had an incentive to speak English well because their goal was to emigrate to the United States. They had never intended England to be their permanent home.

England had been ravaged by the war and was still feeling the effects. America was the land of opportunity where the streets were paved with gold and every able-bodied man could find a job and rise to the top.

As soon as Charles enrolled in English classes, Oskar took him to a Jewish organization asking if they could find him a job. Martin Philipson and Company Ltd., a chemical exporter, hired him to run errands at a salary of 1.15 pounds sterling per week – about US$4.60. His net pay was considerably less after the government deducted income tax. And then Charles also had to pay for the subway and daily lunches. At the end of the week, very little was left. But his English improved rapidly, and the company put him in the office where his job was to send inquiries to chemical manufacturers about their prices. The position came with a raise to 2 pounds sterling per week, about $8 USD.

When the export manager left to work for Electrochemical Industries, a company that manufactured household appliances, he asked Charles to come with him, offering him 4.10 pounds sterling per week.

His new boss suggested they could do some chemical business on the side, so Charles printed up stationary and mailed out inquiries to a few companies he'd dealt with in the past. One day, the president of Oxceda Industries, a Swiss chemical company, knocked on his parents' door. When Terese explained that her son was doing this work "on the side," he told Terese to have Charles call him at his hotel.

He told Charles that he seemed to be an ambitious young man and invited him to dinner so they could talk. He told Charles that he had an office in England run by a finance expert who knew nothing about chemicals. He needed someone who understood the chemical industry and offered Charles 10 pounds sterling per week, adding that Charles could also help himself to an additional 2 pounds sterling per week from petty cash. How he did that, was none of his business. The extra money was tax-free, so its actual worth was more than 4 pounds sterling.

Charles was being paid the equivalent of 15 pounds sterling per week, an exceptionally handsome sum at that time. Not too surprisingly, Oxceda Industries was engaged in shady deals. One, involving the sale of linseed oil from Uruguay to Czechoslovakia, had an outstanding letter of credit for 100,000 pounds sterling, which sat dormant because they couldn't satisfy the currency requirements to get the money.

Charles had always been honest and ethical. He'd been taught those values growing up and had never lost them, so he was disheartened when he discovered the shenanigans going on, especially because he'd been so pleased about finding this great opportunity.

However, he comforted himself with knowing he'd be leaving soon. He was already in touch with Terese's brother, Eugene, who lived in Philadelphia, and with Oskar's niece, Jean, in New York. With his uncle and cousin sponsoring him, a new promised land was quickly becoming a reality.

Two years after arriving in England, Charles set sail for New York.

Chapter 6

NEW YORK

Like most immigrants to America, Charles was greeted by the sight of the Statue of Liberty, holding her torch high in the harbor, welcoming the poor, the homeless, and the desperate, offering them a chance to live the life of their dreams.

Like most, my father surely must have felt a lump in his throat, knowing that the life he wanted for himself was about to begin at last.

He found a hotel room and then a small apartment in Washington Heights, an area in northern Manhattan that became known as Frankfurt on the Hudson due to its large population of German and Austrian Jews. Steven M. Lowenstein picked up on that widely accepted label, publishing a book of that name in 1989.

As soon as Charles was settled, his Uncle Eugene invited him to Philadelphia. While he was there, one of his cousins asked him to dinner. The cousin's daughter's husband had some distant relatives in New York who were in the chemical business, and he offered to introduce Charles.

They, in turn, connected Charles to Hans Schlesinger who was running the European Chemical Company owned by his wife's family in Sweden. Charles met with Schlesinger and one other man who told Charles that business was poor and they were trying to cut expenses. Charles let them know he had both contacts and experience in the chemical industry and thought he could bring in new business.

They offered him a job paying fifty-five dollars per week plus ten percent of the profits from any business he generated. Charles decided that was a generous offer. His expenses were low, the apartment costing only ten dollars per week, the subway ten cents, and lunch twenty-five cents.

In October, they told him that business was so bad, they could no longer afford to keep him on staff. Since he had no other opportunities, Charles made them a counteroffer: keep him on with no salary but pay him one-third of all profits on the business he brought in. They agreed.

In April 1950, Schlesinger told Charles he was unhappy in his work, as was his colleague, Ed Gallard, and so they planned to form their own company. Would Charles like to join them? Their proposal included a weekly salary of seventy-five dollars plus fifteen percent of the net profit of the company, to be paid at the end of the year. Charles thought it was a generous offer, and in June 1950, he began his decades-long career with Gallard-Schlesinger.

By then, the Korean War had started and there was a need for penicillin and other antibiotics. Gallard-Schlesinger had access to these bulk drugs, which they obtained from Pfizer and sold at a huge markup, exporting them all over the world. That profitable business got the company off the ground.

Meanwhile, Charles had become a U.S. citizen and got drafted, but during his medical exam, the doctors gave him a draft deferral because they found a hernia that Charles was completely unaware of. He spent those war years working hard to help make Gallard-Schlesinger a success.

Charles' parents arrived in New York in April 1949, moving in with him until they got an apartment in Manhattan at 790 Riverside Drive. Charles lived with them, but his social life revolved around the New World Club, a social organization of German-Jewish refugees. A good number of refugees were happy to remain part of that diaspora, while others were more eager to assimilate and become fully "Americanized." Charles tended to walk a middle path, fully embracing his new country and everything it stood for, while also enjoying the comfort of a culture he was familiar with. Interestingly, no matter which side of the divide people fell on, they spoke English when they got together. Even if they missed "the old country," they seemed prepared to assimilate and take advantage of their good fortune.

Through the social club, Charles reconnected with some people he had known in France and Switzerland, including Ruth Schloss who was working in a jewelry store. She told Charles about Geraldine (Gerry), who worked in her department. She was single, Ruth said, and pretty, and Charles would probably like her.

Charles lost no time calling her. After all the years of running, hiding, and moving, he'd had no chance to have a real girlfriend, and he was ready. It was clearly one of the best blind dates in the neighborhood that year because three months later he proposed. I can imagine his reaction when he first saw her. She was petite – only 5'2" – and slim with an engaging smile that reached big brown eyes that sparked with a certain mischievous glint. Her dark hair was smoothed back from her face, curling down her neck. She was the first American-born girl he had dated, and in some ways, she was a revelation. She knew very little about the world beyond the United States, never having traveled farther than Florida and Nevada. And she was so American, so alive – so shining – no trace of trauma or sorrow. He was smitten, and clearly, so was she because when he asked her to marry him, she said yes.

Charles was almost dancing with excitement as he drove home to tell his parents. Oskar and Terese didn't share his joy. They liked Gerry but they had wanted Charles to marry a German-Jewish refugee girl. Gerry's family wasn't thrilled either. Paulie, one of Gerry's aunts, said "But he's a foreigner!"

Both families reconciled themselves to the inevitability of the union and accepted it with good grace. Charles and Gerry were married on December 22, 1951, in the rabbi's study at Temple Emanuel in New York. It was a small ceremony with a dinner party reception at Pierre's, a restaurant in New York. The guests included Oskar and Terese and Geraldine's mother, brother, and aunt. With the knot firmly tied, Charles and Gerry moved into their new apartment in the Forest Hills neighborhood in Queens.

After the wedding, Gerry went to work on "Americanizing" Charles with the idea that it would help make him more successful. She had great confidence in his capabilities and business acumen. Charles put up no resistance. He was ready to fully assimilate. By the time I was old enough to make such distinctions, I had no sense that he was anything other than an American.

Gerry was deeply attached to her mother, Lizzie, and wasn't happy living in the apartment in Forest Hills so far from her. She wanted to move in with her mother who lived in Laurelton, a neighborhood in Queens. Because Charles genuinely liked Lizzie, he readily agreed.

Meanwhile, Gallard-Schlesinger moved their office to a building they bought in Long Island City. With no public transportation handy, Charles drove a company car to work, picking up Ed Gallard and Hans Schlesinger, every morning on his way. When they got fed up with the long commute, the partners moved the office to Garden City, a suburb of New York on Long Island. Several years later, they needed more space and bought another building on Long Island in Carle Place.

Charles' and Gerry's first child, Larry, was born September 25, 1952, almost exactly nine months after their wedding. I was born three years later on August 19, 1955. Four years after that, we moved to 821 Newburg Avenue in North Woodmere, the house where I grew up.

It was a house my parents bought "by accident." They were out for a leisurely drive one Sunday when they passed a real estate development featuring seven model homes. On a whim, they decided to take a look. Gerry liked one of the models and Charles asked her if she wanted to buy it. She said yes, they put down a deposit, and just like that, they owned a house. When we moved, Lizzie came with us. None of us would have had it any other way.

I wish I had clearer memories of my grandmother, Lizzie, but it wasn't too long after our move that she had to move into a care facility. At the time, the doctors said she was senile. Today the diagnosis would probably be Alzheimer's. She died in 1964.

My father was good to Lizzie. He was, quite simply, a good guy, but he could also be tough. My aunt told me he had a temper that had toned down over the years. I can remember three times he yelled at me and I was so terrified, I wished he'd hit me with a belt instead – it would have been less painful.

There were arguments in the house too. He and my mother used to fight a lot about money. She didn't grow up with any sort of affluence, but she liked to spend. My father thought she was spend-thrifty and didn't have an accurate handle on how much money they had. I suspect the truth was somewhere in the middle. He probably could have afforded to spend a bit more and she could likely have been a bit more careful.

He was frugal, even when it came to necessities. At the beginning of the school year when my mother took Larry and me shopping for new clothes, he would question the necessity.

Charles had not grown up poor, but I suspect his parents had been quite frugal. When I was a child, I remember my grandmother, Terese, going to the bakery where they would tie up the box of cookies with string. My grandmother would keep the string and reuse it. It's also possible the great deprivation my father experienced, especially during those last years in France, made him careful. When was the next time he might not have enough?

I remember one time in particular when he was furious. Although my mother was Jewish, she had never been a member of a synagogue, nor did she observe the holidays – but she loved Christmas. One December, she bought a miniature Christmas tree, a bag full of tiny ornaments, and a package of shiny silver icicles. We spent the afternoon decorating the tree until we heard my father's car pull into the driveway.

My mother jumped up. "Quick! Hide the tree!"

We shoved it into the closet, dropping icicles on the carpet along the way – no time to pick them up. My father opened the front door, stepped inside, and immediately spotted the silver strands. He followed the trail to the closet, opened the door, and started to steam. I swear, there may have been smoke coming out of his ears. If bodies could be described as exploding, that's pretty much what happened. He was furious, his voice rising a hundred decibels.

Larry and I cowered in our bedroom.

My father was not a religious man. Why such outsized anger? I can only speculate that the tree triggered memories or associations. Christmas meant Christians, supposedly God-fearing people who had persecuted the Jews and had robbed him of so much of his life. Even before the war had started, the children at school had bullied him. They put up Christmas trees, didn't they? But the symbolism meant nothing to them. They were celebrating the birth of a Jewish child. In retrospect, it's easier to understand his anger.

I don't think my mother ever understood. She might tell us, "We have to make allowances for everything your father went through," I don't think she got it at an emotional level. He had been in the thick of the war, fearing for his life almost every day. As a teenager, the war was a story she was told about something that was happening far away.

On the surface, I had a normal childhood. We had a nice house and enough food. I went to school, I had friends, and I played in team sports. My mother didn't work and had time to dedicate herself to us. My father worked long hours. He'd go to the office early in the morning, come home, have dinner, and go downstairs to his den where he would continue working until it was time for bed.

We saw even less of him when he traveled – and he traveled often, particularly to Europe. We lived about twenty minutes from John F. Kennedy International Airport and it seemed we were constantly either dropping him off or picking him up. When I was four, he had to spend three months in Asia. I know it was hard on my mother, but I almost didn't notice, because even when he was home, he was absent.

He often traveled to France and Germany. I would have thought that would be triggering for him and that he would be angry or sad. But years later when I went with him to those countries and asked him, he said, "No. The Germans today are not those who perpetrated the atrocities."

I wonder too, if he put up emotional walls. I know he didn't like to speak German, saying he was rusty and had forgotten most of it. And yet, he still spoke perfect French. He had a sales agent in Germany who said my father spoke perfect German.

He loved speaking French, and I've speculated that he may have associated the language with saving his life. When he moved to Dallas to be close to us after my mother died, he joined a French expat club where they would have potluck dinners once a week at someone's house and everyone spoke only French.

My father wasn't the kind of guy who spent time with us or hugged us, and oh how I longed for that. For him, the most important thing he could do was earn a living. When I was Piggie number three in The Three Little Pigs in my first-grade play, he didn't come to see me. When I graduated from sixth grade, which was a big deal for me, he was attending a large trade show in Germany and didn't come to the ceremony. That hurt more than I like to admit. He didn't come to my high school graduation and I of course would have liked to have had him there.

Once, when I was eight and my father was away, I was lying on the bed with my mother watching television. A commercial for Noxzema shaving cream came on. A little girl was riding around on a tricycle in front of her house. Her father pulled into the driveway, got out of the car, and scooped her up, holding her tight, big smiles on both their faces. I started to cry. "Mommy," I said, wiping tears away. "Why can't daddy be more like that?"

My mother understood my hurt. She wanted my father to be different but felt incapable of changing him.

When I was eleven or twelve, a Boy Scout in sixth grade, I was to be named a Tenderfoot in a special ceremony with two other boys. Mr. Barash, the scoutmaster, asked the boys to bring their fathers. Of course, my father was not about to come. He had to work.

My mother dropped me off at the ceremony. Mr. Barash called us up to the front of the room. Then he said, "I want your fathers to join you."

I turned to him. "Mr. Barash, my father's not here. He couldn't make it."

"He's not?"

In that brief pause, I turned back to the people sitting in front of me – and there was my father, walking up the aisle toward me.

The memory still brings tears, even though I suspect my mother tore into him and told him, "What's wrong with you? You have to go. It will only take fifteen minutes."

That moment, seeing him there just for me, lit me up inside like a megawatt candle.

As the years went by, he mellowed and softened. We started hugging. He'd hug me every time I left the house to go back to college, or whenever I came home. He never said, "I love you," but we embraced.

More than anything. I wanted him to be proud of me.

Chapter 7

TURNING POINT

When I graduated from college, I taught high school math for two years in Nicaragua and one year in Colombia. That last year, my father suggested we meet in San Juan, Puerto Rico over the Christmas holidays.

I didn't have a telephone, so we communicated via telex. My father had a machine in his office and he would send messages to the one in my local post office. The post office would then call the school where I was teaching, "We have a message for Mr. Schwarz."

On my way home from school, I would pick it up. In our back-and-forth correspondence, we embarked on a political discussion, and he wrote, "This is a hard place to have this conversation. We can continue it on the beach in Puerto Rico."

I was unreasonably excited and filled with hope. I conjured an image of an intimate stroll along the beach with my dad, maybe in the late afternoon, the sun beginning to dip toward the water, talking and exchanging ideas, having his full attention focused on me and caring about what I had to say.

That never happened.

As a kid, I loved baseball. My dad didn't understand the game and he didn't really care. I desperately wanted to go out in the front yard with him and throw the baseball around. Of course, that never happened either.

A movie I love is Field of Dreams starring Kevin Costner. There's a scene with Kevin Costner's dad as a young man, and Kevin says to him, "Hey dad, you wanna have a catch?"

Just thinking about that scene brings up deep emotions. That is everything I ever wanted as a kid growing up.

I was in my late thirties when my wife, my kids, and I were in California, visiting my wife's sister. Early on Sunday I returned to Dallas alone and had dinner with my father. It was just an ordinary meal. We were digging in and my father was talking. I don't even remember what the subject was, but a thought exploded across my mind. "Holy shit! I'm not afraid of you anymore!"

That in itself might not seem like an epiphany – but what was remarkable was that until that moment, I hadn't realized I was afraid of him. The shock and blessing were in seeing the fear evaporate. Recognizing it, made it vanish. Human emotional development is complex. I was never sure what I was afraid of; he never hit me and rarely if ever punished me. But he seemed larger than life to me.

The event was transformative. I understood for the first time how much of my behavior had been centered on making him proud of me. It had always been an elusive goal at best, because he never said, "I'm proud of you." He never gave praise. He never said, "I love you. You make me happy." When the "fear of him" evaporated, I was free to be more of my true self following my own dreams and setting my own goals.

That was the turning point where I started living my life for me, and that of course, was the real beginning of a great relationship with him. He had never been unwilling; he had been incapable, and I was able to fully internalize that distinction.

Can I trace all my father's behaviors back to the Holocaust, his separation from his parents at thirteen, and the harrowing years that followed? Probably not. The culture he grew up in was formative. His father, Oskar, was also not demonstrative. And yet, there were those nights in France where he cried himself to sleep. Those war years changed his life.

By the time my father died in 2007, we had a wonderful relationship. I took what he was able to give, knowing it was the best he could do, and it was enough. I had stopped yearning for more. During those good years with him, I learned so much. He never stopped surprising me. One day we were having lunch and he asked, "What did you do last night?"

"I went to the opera."

"What opera did you see?"

"La Bohème."

"Who did you go with?"

"I went alone."

"Why did you go alone?"

"Robin doesn't like the opera and I don't have anyone to go with, so I go alone."

"Why didn't you invite me?"

I paused a moment. "You like the opera?"

"I love the opera!"

"Dad! I had no idea you liked the opera!"

"Yeah, I used to go as a boy. I love it."

Well then! And so we got season tickets to the opera and had wonderful nights together.

My father was a man who at some point decided emotions weren't important. He believed he had to achieve and become successful. But as the years went by, those deep emotions found more room for expression.

I have a memory of a time my father absolutely surprised me. My mother often pestered my father, "Charles, let's go out. Let's travel."

His answer was almost invariably, "No, I can't I have to work."

My mother died in 1987, and we sat shiva, a Jewish ritual that involved a week of mourning and observances after the burial of a close relative. We observed Shiva for two nights. Everyone loved my mother, and they all came to the house to pay their respects. On the first night, we were sitting in the living room talking, and I looked over at my father who was holding court, telling stories and fully engaging all the attention in the room. I was stunned. "Where have you been for thirty years? I didn't know you had this in you. Why weren't you more like this with mom?"

Dad moved to Dallas when my kids, Aaron and Rachel, were fifteen months old. He attended every sports event and every school occasion. He went to Aaron's hockey games and Rachel's volleyball games even if he had no clue about the rules or what was happening on the playing field. He came to my daughter's ballet recitals – he never missed a thing. I wondered one day if it was possible, even just once, that while he was watching my son play, he didn't perhaps see me on the ice in place of Aaron.

At my dad's funeral, my son talked about how important it had been to him that his grandfather showed up. My grandson's middle name is Charles. My father may not have shown it, but he had a good heart. We have a tradition in Jewish culture call "L'dor v'dor." It means "from generation to generation" and is all about passing down learning, teaching and customs from one generation to the next. Naming my grandson "Charles" is a great example of L'dor v'dor.

I miss him. There are times when a problem smacks me in the face and I wonder, "What would my father say?"

His death was no surprise, but even being prepared for it, it still came as a shock. We did everything we could to honor him at his funeral and during the days that immediately followed. His family and all his friends came back to the house after the funeral. We told stories and toasted him with endless glasses of wine, which is exactly what he would have wanted us to do.

I told my favorite Charles story:

When I was a kid, my friends used to sleep over. On the weekends, my mother let us stay up as late as we wanted. We'd played games like Monopoly, Risk, Life, or Stratego in my bedroom, across the hall from my parents' room. My father would be asleep while my mother watched TV in the living room. There were times our play would get a bit raucous and my mother would come down the hall, open the door, and say, "Shhh, you're going to wake your father."

We'd tone it down and continue playing. That pattern repeated itself for years. Always the footsteps down the hall, the door opening, and, "Shhh, You're going to wake your father."

We did not want to wake my father. We had no idea what the consequences would be, and we didn't want to find out. At some level, there had to be fear.

In my freshman year in college, I was home for Thanksgiving and went out with all the friends I used to have sleepovers with. At 1.30 a.m., I heard the clatter of pebbles hitting my window. I opened the window and looked out – there were my four best friends. I let them in, bringing them up to my room where we started talking and laughing. My mother soon joined us because she loved the activity and could never resist being part of the action.

There were six of us now, and we got a little loud. But even through our noise, we heard the footsteps. We'd woken my father – the sleeping giant!

It got so quiet in my room that you could hear a proverbial pin drop. We looked at each other and my mother. Now what? What was he going to do? A rush of childhood dread crept over us. Our age-old fear was about to materialize.

We heard the footsteps stop at my door. It opened, and there he was, wearing boxers and a T-shirt. He took in the scene and said, "It's three o'clock in the morning!"

Anybody want a beer?"

He disappeared while we stared at each other, jaws quite literally dropped. He came back minutes later with two six packs of beer icy cold from the refrigerator. And there we all were, drinking beer, my father swigging it back with the rest of us.

I think that's when my father decided I was a young man – no longer a child; that I was coming of age.

It's my favorite Charles story, and one of my favorite memories of my father, who was a good man with depths to him I may never fully know.

Chapter 8

AFTERWARDS

Despite the trauma my father experienced growing up, he built a beautiful life for himself and his family in America. Kids are said to be resilient and that they "bounce back." My father didn't bounce back, he bounced forward; from place to place, from situation to situation. He was incredibly resilient.

He left the past behind him, never holding a grudge. If he exploded in anger, it vanished within minutes. It's a trait I'm glad he passed on to me. Like him, I can move forward without regrets and make the best of situations. If things don't go my way, I look for the lesson. My father didn't teach me that, he modeled it.

He had emotional limitations, but he was one of the smartest people I ever knew, and I was lucky enough to get the best of him. Was there some dysfunction in our family? Of course. But it paled in comparison to all that was good.

When my brother and I were growing up, he worked constantly. He had no time for us, but if he ever did express interest in spending time together, I jumped at it. Today, if one of my kids calls me and asks if I'd like to do something with them, "yes" is the only answer. I felt the same about spending time with my father. He had favorite television shows we'd watch together. He would sit in his recliner, and I'd be right there beside him. I would bring a couple of oranges downstairs because he liked oranges, and I'd watch him meticulously peel and section them, sharing them with me. It was such a simple thing, and so meaningful to me.

We'd watch Arrest and Trial and The FBI, two crime dramas from the 1960s. One of his favorite comedies was Hogan's Heroes, also from the 1960s. He'd laugh and laugh, thoroughly enjoying anything that made fun of the Germans.

I'd find almost any excuse for interaction with him. He'd be downstairs working while I was up in my room doing homework, and I'd find a reason to ask him about a problem I was working on. I didn't really need help, but it was a chance to talk to him. In the seventh grade, I had my first opportunity in school to learn another language, While most of my classmates chose Spanish, I opted for French. Now I had a lot of excuses to ask my father for help. Most of the time, I was doing just fine on my own. I suspect he probably knew that and was happy to be complicit in my little charade, knowing it stemmed entirely from my love for him.

Being in business with him was a revelation, raising my respect for him to new levels. As a chemical importer, he needed to know the names and locations of thousands of manufacturers. He had to cross-reference someone in the United States who needed a particular product, with the best manufacturer somewhere in the world. Because there was no readily available resource for the information, he created a directory under a separate company name, cutting my uncle in for twenty-five percent.

Essentially, he had no competition, and the small company became quite successful. In the mid-nineteen-eighties, I was operating a software and programming company, writing software for businesses. By this time my father's directory consisted of five thousand companies and fifty thousand chemicals manually maintained on index cards, all carefully cross-referenced. His book, The Directory of World Chemical Producers, was extremely popular with his clients and others in the chemical industry.

One day, I said, "Dad, I can make your life a lot easier. I can take this and put it into a database on a PC that you can search, add to, and edit."

Absolutely not. Why would he do such a thing?

I kept at him and about two years later, he reluctantly said, "Okay, let's try it."

About nine months after his okay, we had input all the data and written the search software. I asked him to come to my office to show him how it worked. I input a random chemical he might want to search for, hit a key, and showed him the producers. He almost fell off his chair.

"That's it? It's that easy?'

"It's that easy. And here's how you can change it, add chemicals to a company, or add another company."

He didn't throw his sixty thousand index cards out right away, but the computer system changed everything. My father was my client now, but it was much more than just another job. It meant so much to me, to be able to do something for him that was genuinely useful.

In about 1989, before the advent of the internet, my father said, "I'm getting all these faxes from people who want to know if they can buy something electronic instead of the physical book. Can we do that?"

"Yes. Absolutely," I said, outlining the process. He bought in completely.

"I'll make you a deal," he said. "Do the work, and I'll pay your company for it, just like I always have. Or, we'll form a new database company. You work for free and I'll give you one-third of the profits from the database version."

It was one of the hardest decisions I ever made. I had two young kids and couldn't afford not to get paid, and I had no idea if anyone would actually buy an electronic version of the directory. After talking it over with my wife for several days, I finally decided that I liked the product. I knew it was good and viable. If I wasn't going to take this risk, what risk would I ever take?

I told my father, "Yes."

It was the best decision I ever made. I was pulling about six or seven thousand dollars out of the company every month, and in the 1990s, that was a lot of money for me. But it wasn't just the earnings that were important, I also had equity in the company.

My father and I started traveling all over the world together, attending trade shows and meeting interesting people. Some asked for new products, and my head filled with ideas. My father wasn't interested in new products. He was content with what he had, but he was happy to support me.

"Let's form another company," he said. "I want ten percent, give your brother ten percent, and you keep eighty percent, and launch these new products on your own. Good luck."

Over the next few years, we developed four or five new products. None hit it out of the ballpark like the original directory had, but collectively, they did very well.

The best part of the enterprise? I got to work with him. He taught me the chemical and pharmaceutical industry, and I taught him about computers and software. We traveled a great deal together, and sitting beside him on an airplane felt almost as good as being next to his recliner while he peeled oranges.

By 2005, we had merged both companies into one and sold it for a good price. But there was one important proviso. My father was happy to sell the company but wanted to keep working. The deal I negotiated with the buyer included giving him a job in perpetuity. They loved him and were happy to keep him on. Truthfully, it was an excellent deal for them because my father was a brilliant man and a great resource for them. Even though his health had started to fail, he was still a valuable contributor.

One of the first thoughts I had when my father died was, "Oh my God! There is so much knowledge that is not on this earth anymore! Surely the world is going to miss that."

I added, only half-jokingly, "The average intelligence of the world just dropped a little bit."

Chapter 9

GRANDPARENTS

I have wonderful memories of my father, and I also remember my grandparents with great fondness. When I was a boy and we lived on Long Island, my father and I went to their ninth-floor apartment in Manhattan almost every week for Sunday lunch. We'd ring the bell and my grandmother would open the door and give us both big hugs. Then my grandfather would come walking down the long corridor and would shake my father's hand and then mine.

We'd sit down around the kitchen table, where we'd eat cold cuts and bread. But my grandmother was an excellent baker, and that was the highlight of those afternoons. She made an apple pie that was so good, that words can't describe it. I would sometimes call her during the week and say, "Grandma, I'm coming for lunch on Sunday. Can you make apple pie?"

Of course, she always did.

She also made a delicious trifle. I'm pretty sure she learned to make that in England. To this day, when I am invited for dinner and am asked to bring dessert, my choice is often a trifle.

I remember little of what we talked about around the table. Sometimes my father and grandfather would talk about the stock market and investments, and occasionally, my father would help with issues around social security or other government red tape.

When I was in first grade and played the part of Piggie number three in the school play and my father didn't attend, but my grandparents came – all the way from Manhattan to Long Island. When I was eight, they took me to see Oliver, my first Broadway show, which started my lifelong love of theatre.

The war and the antisemitism they endured during those years must have affected them very differently from my father. They were older and more mature. Charles was just a boy. I believe the hardest part for them, especially Terese, was being separated from their son for so long. They lost everything, but they were resilient and rebuilt. Like my father, they bounced forward. I suspect my father inherited or learned that quality from them.

It takes great courage and fortitude to have everything taken from you and then to walk boldly into a future of unknowns in a new country.

The German government paid a lot in reparations to Germans to compensate for what they had lost and what was taken away from them during the Holocaust. They typically paid either a lifetime pension, paid monthly or a lump sum amount. They offered Oskar a lump sum, but he believed he was entitled to a lifetime pension because of how much had been taken from him.

The German government argued that he had replicated and replaced what he had lost when he was in England and wasn't entitled to a lifetime pension. Oskar disagreed with their logic and filed a lawsuit against the German government, which he won and ended up getting his lifetime pension.

Oskar and Terese also filed another lawsuit regarding the apartment building in Ludwigshafen at Gruenerstrasse 1, which Terese had inherited when Carl died. She sold the building in 1938 under duress to Franz Hage and his wife Klara. My grandmother often talked about how the Nazis would come by every day asking her to sell the building and telling her that if she didn't, it would be taken away from her. She finally sold it in 1938 at about fifty percent of its market value.

After the war, the Germans ruled that all contracts entered into under duress were null and void. So in the 1950s, Terese and Oskar sued the Hages to get the building back. The court ruled that the sales contract was null and void and returned the building to them. Unfortunately, it had been bombed by the Allies in 1945, and what they got back was a piece of land with a pile of rubble. However, they were still able to sell it to a real estate developer.

An important postscript to my grandparents' and father's lives is the installation of three stolpersteine in front of their old house in Ludwigshafen.

Stolpersteine means "stumbling stone" and has become a way of remembering Holocaust victims. The stones measure about four-by-four inches with a brass plaque on top and are installed on the sidewalk outside the last place where a Holocaust victim voluntarily lived. A lot of meanings and metaphors exist about stolpersteine. The first is that there used to be an antisemitic trope in Germany that if you were walking down the street and tripped on a cobblestone, they would say "a Jew is buried there." Now, with stolpersteine, we are symbolically burying Jews right there.

Gunter Demnig, the artist who conceived of the Stolperstein project, said there are lots of Holocaust museums and Holocaust memorials, and you can decide if you want to visit them or not. If you don't, they are easy to avoid. But stolpersteine are randomly placed so you can't avoid them. They are embedded into the fabric of the city.

About 90,000 stolperstein are installed throughout Europe, not just in Germany.

In May 2023, stolpersteine were installed for Terese Schwarz, Oskar Schwarz, and Charles Schwarz, aka Karl Sidlin, on the sidewalk outside their last residence at 65 Prinzregentenstrasse in Ludwigshafen.

Chapter 10

THOUGHTS

The holocaust happened eighty years ago. Have we learned the lessons we needed to? Are we better today?

I don't think so.

Hitler didn't invent antisemitism. Jews have been targeted for centuries, and that didn't change after World War II. Antisemitism today is on the rise. Racism probably exists more in America than in other countries around the world, but antisemitism is global.

The United States immigration policy in the 1930s was targeted against Jews because the government was worried they might be German spies. Was that honestly the reason? Almost a hundred years later, not much has changed in that regard. I don't think we've advanced or solved the problem.

Could it happen again? I've always believed it could not – certainly not in America. But I changed my mind when I saw that hate crimes against Jews between 2017 and 2021 had increased by more than four hundred percent. And then, after the October 7 attack in Israel, hate crimes against Jews skyrocketed even more. These are from statistics published by the Department of Justice and the Southern Poverty Law Center. I was stunned when, in response to a Nazi march in Charlottesville, Virginia, the President of the United States said, "There are good people on both sides."

There are not. If you're a Nazi, you're not a good person.

It seems a platform of hate and antisemitic behavior has become acceptable.

I don't know if it could happen in the same way again. I doubt there would be concentration camps and ovens burning bodies by the thousands. If there is another disaster for Jews, it will likely be more subtle. Other ethnic and religious groups are having far more children than Jews. They will outnumber Jews at the voting booths. Will they vote for politicians that support issues that are unfavorable to Jews? I don't know but I do think about this.

I look at the rise of Christian Nationalism that is trying to turn America into a Christian theocracy. The Texas Supreme Court ruled that public schools can teach the Bible if it's an academic exercise, but that's not what is happening in practice. Public schools are teaching creationism. I wouldn't want my kids going to that school. I don't even want my kids going to a public school where they're teaching Jewish theology. We have to keep a separation between church and state.

Politicians want to get elected. They will appeal to the largest voting bloc. This is one of the things that makes the existence of Israel so important. I don't want to leave America. I love my country. I recognize a lot of its problems and faults, but it's my home. Still, it's reassuring to know that I always have a place to go where I will be safe.

The Germans willingly gave up their rights to Hitler. It was a democratic country – a sovereign nation. They drank the Kool-Aid and decided that Hitler's policies were going to make Germany better.

We can't follow that path. Democracy flourishes when we listen to and accept, even embrace, individual opinions and the right to express them. But both the left and the right are guilty of condemning those who don't hold their views. It has to stop.

I've been giving presentations about my father and the Holocaust for years. Why? Because we know that people who have learned about the Holocaust are far less likely to be antisemitic. My goal is to educate them. My father's is only one story, but I hope it resonates enough that when they hear someone say, "Those stupid cheap Jews," they'll stop them and tell them why that's wrong.

Every time I give a presentation with video clips of my father, I feel like I am honoring him – and he deserves that.

If you're an American, I want to point you to a three-part documentary miniseries, The U.S. and the Holocaust. Produced in 2022 by Ken Burns, it's about the United States' response to the Holocaust. While it talks about the atrocities in Germany, its main focus is on what was occurring in America. What was the political response? What was the public saying and thinking? How did they feel about increasing Jewish immigration?

I can tell you this: the documentary will not make you proud to be an American. Most startling perhaps was the Nazi rally that took place in Madison Square Gardens in New York on February 20, 1939. More than twenty thousand people attended. The stage at the event featured a huge portrait of George Washington with swastikas on each side.

During that time, Camp Siegfried, a summer camp located in Yaphank, New York, on Long Island, taught Nazi ideology. It was owned by the German American Bund, an American Nazi organization devoted to promoting a favorable view of Nazi Germany, and was operated by the German American Settlement League (GASL).

I believe the antidote to antisemitism is education and information, and yet even this most valuable tool is being undermined. Recently, the University of Texas' Board of Regents announced that young people admitted to the university whose family's income is less than $100,000, will be eligible for free tuition and fees. The Texas legislature pushed back. One lawmaker said, "This is un-American. Nothing is free here. This is communism. What are we doing? This is overreach by unelected officials who don't understand how the world works."

My answer to that is, "What? Who would deny someone the opportunity to go to college for free? Why is that not a great thing?"

It is easier to feed false information or to withhold information from people who are not educated and don't understand critical thinking.

Maybe I can't change the world with my presentation, with my book, or with my unflagging advocacy. But I will never stop trying to educate and enlighten whenever and wherever I can. I know it makes a difference.

I hope you will take what you have learned here and make a difference too.

EPILOGUE

There are a few takeaways from Charles' story. The first is a message of hopefulness. Despite the trauma and hardship he experienced as a child, he built a beautiful life in America for himself and his family. When I was growing up and hit rough spots, I could look back at my father's tumultuous story and say to myself that nothing I could possibly experience would ever compare. "Dad got through it. I can get through it." My father's story gave me hope and strength.

Another takeaway is that "silence is complicity." Most people's moral compasses are not defective. We know when something is wrong. We can identify evil. When we do, we must react, whether it's a bully on a playground or a news anchor embracing Nazis. We have to speak up and say, "This isn't okay." When the Hages "bought" my grandparent's apartment building on Gruenerstrasse 1 for half its market value because they were Jews, they had to know that what they were doing was wrong, immoral, and unethical.

Before the Holocaust, Germany enacted many decrees that humiliated, marginalized, and impoverished the Jews. People remained silent. They accepted the decrees as normal. The Holocaust may never have occurred if people had spoken up. They didn't. Martin Niemoller, a German theologian and Lutheran pastor who did speak up and opposed the Nazis in the late 1930s said:

- First, they came for the socialists, and I did not speak out—because I was not a socialist.
- Then they came for the trade unionists, and I did not speak out—because I was not a trade unionist.

- Then they came for the Jews, and I did not speak out—because I was not a Jew.
- Then they came for me—and there was no one left to speak for me.

The quote expresses the belief that Germans were complicit through their silence. He felt this was especially true about the leaders of the Protestant churches.

The last takeaway is a set of ethical but rhetorical questions to ponder. These questions were posited by Gloria DeVidas Kirchheimer and Manfred Kirchheimer in their book, We Were So Beloved about the German Jewish community of Washington Heights in New York City. They are:

- Are there lessons in survival?
- Do people change?
- Do survivors have any special obligations?
- What about feelings of collective guilt?

WHY THE JEWS?

Where did antisemitism come from?

I speak all over the country, telling my father's and grandparents' story of survival. The question I probably get asked most often is, "Why the Jews?" And so, I want to briefly address that question.

Thousands and probably millions of words have been written about antisemitism. Entire courses on the subject are taught at universities around the world. While it's not possible to do the question complete justice in a short space, I'll do my best to speak to it.

After Jesus was born, he and his disciples preached his message and revelations. They were widely accepted and led to many people adopting Christianity. However, the Jews did not accept those teachings. They had their own set of beliefs laid out in the Talmud and the Old Testament. They weren't interested in these new "revelations."

The Jewish position was largely accepted. Christians didn't pressure them to convert, but as the two groups diverged over the next few hundred years, several myths about the Jews developed.

The first was that the Jews killed Jesus. We know they did not. The Romans killed Jesus, but the erroneous belief was widely held regardless.

The second myth was called "blood liable." This was the belief that Jews were kidnapping Christian babies and using their blood for ritualistic purposes. The most current version is that Jews mixed Christian blood with Passover unleavened bread. But there are older versions of the legend. Medieval and Eastern European sources sometimes state that the wound of circumcision does not heal unless it is washed with Christian blood. Or that Jews are condemned to suffer in perpetuity from hemorrhoids after the killing of Jesus, and only potions based on Christian blood may heal them. Another variant claims that after the death of Jesus, Jewish men, as well as women, menstruate until they drink the blood of a Christian victim. In yet another version, Christian blood is supposed to free Jews from eye infections and is to be used to make powerful love potions. It is even supposed to rid Jews of a unique odor that non-Jews use to identify them, an odor that can't be eradicated any other way.

There are two decisive arguments for excluding any kernel of truth in connection with these legends. The first concerns blood in general, and the second is Christian blood specifically. The taboo against the consumption of blood is one of the strongest and most characteristic taboos of the Jewish religion. In Genesis 9:4, God enjoins Noah and his sons: "You shall not eat flesh with its life, that is, its blood." And Moses is commanded in Leviticus 7:26–27: "You shall not eat any blood in any of your dwellings, whether of bird or beast. Whoever eats any blood, that person shall be cut off from his people." Leviticus 17:10–14 presents the prohibition even more extensively, and the injunction is reconfirmed in Deuteronomy 12:23, "Only be sure that you do not eat the blood, for the blood is the life."

As Jews and Christians were largely segregated, not because of hate but because they now shared different religious views, these myths became indoctrinated into Christian thought. Moreover, it was difficult to create friendships because they couldn't eat together. Jews had strict dietary laws with most keeping Kosher. They didn't eat pork or seafood and didn't combine dairy with meat. So, it was difficult to socialize if people couldn't share meals together.

And so, Christians didn't get to know Jews on any kind of deeply personal level, and the myths perpetuated. Two of the earliest universities founded in the English-speaking world, Oxford (1096 AD) and Cambridge (1209 AD), were deeply connected to the church. As you can imagine, the church wasn't very interested in dispelling the myths against Jews, so the truth wasn't being taught at Oxford and Cambridge. Therefore, the myths continued to live on and became more and more embedded in Christian culture.

Around the same time, at approximately 1100 AD, you start to see restrictions on Jewish life concerning the types of jobs they are allowed to have. They were prevented from having businesses in certain industries, which explains why so many became merchants and traders. This helped to further develop the antisemitic attitudes towards Jews, and they were marginalized even more.

This state of things continued until approximately 1800 AD when the mayor of Vienna realized they were losing a lot of tax revenue by restricting the jobs Jews could hold, so he lifted the restrictions on them. It is important to note that this was based solely on the financial situation and wasn't an act of humanism or empathy.

For the next 130 years, the Jewish community in Europe flourished. For the first time, they could work wherever they chose, until Hitler came to power in Germany in 1933 and pointed to the Jews as the reason for Germany's economic problems. He also blamed the Jews for Germany's humiliating defeat in World War I.

Despite countless persecutions over thousands of years, Jews have survived. I have no doubt that we will continue to survive. But if we are to see permanent change in attitudes toward Jews, we have to teach this history. Knowledge and information are the antidote to hate. And that makes it all seem pretty easy to do.

ACKNOWLEDGMENTS

Charlotte Decoster at the Dallas Holocaust and Human Rights Museum recruited me as a speaker some years ago, and while telling her my father's story, she showed me that there were still many documents out there about him and my grandparents. She got me thinking differently about his story. Growing up, it was almost a fable. She inspired me to think about it academically, and it set me on a mission to learn more and to document what I discovered. As a result, I have gathered hundreds and hundreds of pages of original documents from the 1920s, 1930s, and 1940s from France, Switzerland, Germany, and England, and I now know more about my father's story than he ever did. This book would not have been written without her.

I also want to acknowledge Stefan Moerz, director of the municipal archives in Ludwigshafen, who got interested and passionate about my family's history and dug up hundreds of documents about them. He also spearheaded the installation of the stolpersteine.

Thank you to Trisha Murphy, then a graduate student at the University of Texas at Dallas. who on her own, contacted the Swiss authorities to see what documents they had about my father. They returned eighty-eight different documents!

I am grateful to the faculty at the Ackerman Center for Holocaust Studies at the University of Texas at Dallas who were so happy to answer the hundreds of questions that came up about the Holocaust.

I want to thank my children, Aaron and Rachel Schwarz, who love the legacy their grandfather left, and have promised to continue teaching it and speaking long after I'm gone. They continue to be an inspiration to me.

Lastly, I am indebted to the staff at the resource center at the Memorial de la Shoah in Paris who helped me gather many, many documents about my father's 3 ½ years in France.

All of you helped make this book a reality.

ABOUT THE AUTHOR

Ron Schwarz lives in Dallas, Texas, and Park City, Utah. When he's not speaking and teaching about the Holocaust, he loves to ski, play golf, tennis, and pickleball, and ride his bike. He loves good food, whiskey, and great wine, particularly heavy reds. He's partial to Italian wines but enjoys them all – he's an equal-opportunity drinker who doesn't discriminate based on origin or color. He loves to travel and has been all over the world. People ask him all the time where the one place is that he thinks is the best, but it's an impossible question to answer. Every country and city has something special to offer, and you never know exactly what you'll find that will resonate with you.

He has visited 47 out of the 50 states, so he's looking forward to knock out those remaining three: North Dakota, South Dakota, and Alaska. He works in the information services area and owns two companies: one that publishes directories for the legal sector and another that publishes different databases for the pharmaceutical industry. He serves on an advisory board to the Dean of the School of Education at the University of Wisconsin and also on the advisory council to the Director of the Ackerman Center for Holocaust Studies at the University of Texas at Dallas. He speaks Spanish and French very well. He loves, loves, loves dogs and believes they embody the characteristics that we should all aspire to: genuineness, authenticity, love, and loyalty. He has two children; boy/girl twins, and two grandchildren. And while he loves his children unconditionally, his heart explodes when he sees his grandkids.

PHOTOS AND DOCUMENTS

Photos, Documents and Videos are also available at:

https://www.ronschwarz.com/documents-and-videos

Krudepils
Dnuutze з ;tains

f52

fastvadi9241;

edle«

ustpit

itecitt la et,

&α

g
rie kＺeinet* itereit-tx/ g (ＺU/Ｓet
erat eftx eneletety kᵢ, ldee raz-
tiAte] Ｌ℮⁻ fre e-
21ro%a4a Ｚ# LUlms dittatitt,
Mapittil: 7/0 stel, leere ner /egg,"
tg&

ＯtＡr ardk Ａtte
1&

Certificate from Carl's rabbi in Latvia stating that Carl is from Latvia and is the son of Shlom Berk Sidlin and his wife Dina Sidlin (Original in Latvian).

Rabbi of the Krustpils Jewish Parish	**CERTIFICATE**
January 2, 1925	This certificate is issued to the citizen of
No. 1	Kreslava Mr. Shlom Berk Sidlin [Šļom Berk
in Krustpils City	Sidlin] and his wife Mrs. Dina, the daughter of
[A stamp: Latvia, 40 santims, 2/1 1925]	Arons, surname before wedlock Murin on this tenth day of September 1889 in order to certify that they had a son who was given a name Calke Cari Karl, which fact is duly certified by my personal signature and seal.

Rabbi of the Krustpils Parish

/signature illegible/

[Round stamp: the emblem of the parish, Rabbi of the Krustpils Parish]

Certificate from Carl's rabbi in Latvia stating that Carl is from Latvia and is the son of Shlom Berk Sidlin and his wife Dina Sidlin (English translation).

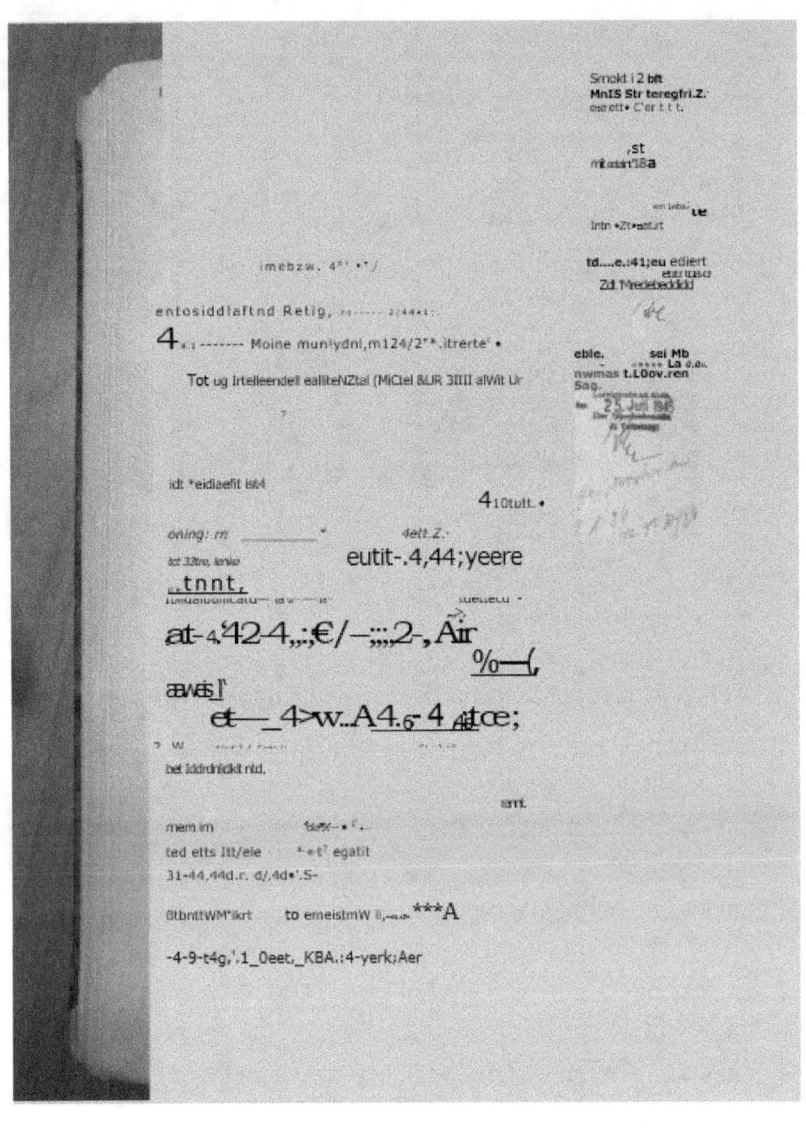

Carl and Terese Marriage Certificate (Original in German).

No. *126*

(Notice of Intended Marriage Register No. *79*.)

Ludwigshafen on the Rhine, on _____ *seventeenth of* _____
Marc h _____ nineteen hundred *twen ty five.*

Before the signed registrar appeared today for the purpose of marriage:

1. the *watchmaker Zalke (Karl) Sidlin,* _____

The personality known as ....

born on _____ *tenth of September*

of the year _____ *eighteen* hundred *eig h ty n in e*

in *Kreuzburg, Lettland,* _____

birth register _____ of the registrar in *otherw is e provided birth*
certificate of the rabbinate in Kreuzburg;
resid in g in Ludwigshafen, Prinzregenten strasse 68 _____ ;

    2. the *unreadable Therese Marx,*

The personality known as _____

born on _____ *tw elf th of May*

of the year _____)) _____ *n in e te en* hundred _____

in *Ralingen, district Trier,* _____

birth register No. *1 9* of the registrar in *We lsch billig*

residing in *Saarbrücken, unreadable 1;* _____

According to § 2 of the 2nd
Ordinance on the Implementation
of the Act on the Change of
Surname and Given Names of
August 17th 1938 the mentioned
Therese born Marx with effect
from January 1st 1939 she has
adopted the additional first name
Sara unreadable. Ludwigshafen
on the Rhine, on *December 28th*
1938
      The registrar
      on behalf
      unreadable

The above marginal note is deleted in
accordance with Law No. 1 of the US
Military Government.
    Ludwigshafen on the
    Rhine on July 25th
    1945 The registrar
    on behalf of
    unreadable

Carl and Terese Marriage Certificate (English Translation)

View of Prinzregentenstrasse in the 1920s. The watchmaker shop is on the right where the clock is.

Fachgelehält für Uhren, Gold- und Silberwaren

111.111111R 11171
latedgetden Eth.

CARL S1DLIN

Bak -Lotte:
DRESDNER ORME
taiwemhdee•

wen C CNORMAHH

11äteddl ane CesalAs polellaalloadaRell 01.•blat Os) IX

Ludwigshafen a. Rk. Prisaregentenitraße 6$

FERNSPRECHER Nr. 561

Rechnung ws,   tut- rts.,e,tat

ti•la

Ha..44444",, ,Are tet

der —
met
e₁***ne —***

'   -

-

Invoice from Carl's watchmaker shop from January 13, 1922. (Original in German).

Ludwigshafen o. Rh., on June 13, 1922

Specialist Dealer for Watches, Gold- and Silverware

Postal Check Account: Number 11871 Ludwigshafen o. Rh.	CARL SIDLIN formerly C. CHORMANN	Bank Account: DRESDNER BANK Ludwigshafen o. Rh.

Member of the German Precision-Watchfactory Glashuette (Sa.) e. G. m. b. H.

Ludwigshafen o. Rh., Prinzregentenstrasse 68
TELEPHONE Nr. 568

Invoice for *Mister Otto Feuschel (?)*
unreadable

June 13, 1922	House clock No. 2308 [in treatment](?) On account	6800 .- 2000 .-
Carl Sidlin formerly Carl Chormann Ludwigshafen o. Rh.	*Remain* *Carl Sidlin*	4800 .-

Invoice from Carl's watchmaker shop from January 13, 1922. (English translation).

Eine furchtbare Bluttat

Zwei Tote und zwei Verletzte in der Prinzregentenstraße.

Newspaper article about the murder of Carl Sidlin: January 12, 1926 (Original in German).

A Terrible Bloody Act
Two dead and two injured at Prinzregentenstrasse.

A terrible bloody act took place yesterday afternoon at Prinzregentenstraße 68. Shortly after 2 o'clock in Karl Sidlin's gold ware and watch dealer store the watchmaker assistant Weise appeared and asked for work from Sidlin. Weise recently worked for Sidlin as a watchmaker; Sidlin hired him at yesterday's interview again for the beginning of next week. The conversation between Weise and Sidlin took place in the workshop, with watchmaker assistant Hinlang present.

Suddenly, Weise drew a gun and started shooting blindly without any reason. A shot hit Sidlin in the back of the head, pierced his head and came out under his nose. Sidlin was also dead at once. Then Weise shot at the saleswoman Miss Lemke, Sidlin's employee, who was present in the store. He shot her right lower leg and seriously injured her. Then the murderer fired at watchmaker Hinlang, who had taken refuge behind a cupboard. A bullet brushed Hinlang's left hip, injuring only the skin. As a result, the offender Weise went into the store and killed himself by a shot in the right temple. He, too, was dead on the spot. Seven minutes had passed from Weise's entrance to the terrible bloody deed.

The content of various cards from Weise left behind, suggest that the offender was insane. The criminal police appeared immediately after the deed at the crime scene. They blocked the crime scene until court commission has recorded the facts.

The reasons for this terrible act can not yet be stated. The investigations by the Criminal Investigation Department in this direction are ongoing and should provide further clarity. Whether it is an act of revenge or whether there are private disputes is still unclear.

The watchmaker Sidlin had joined Thormann's business a few years ago as an assistant, and then took over the business himself. He has been married for a year and has been the father of an 8 day old boy. The wife is in the gynecological clinic of the municipal hospital and knew nothing about her husband's death by the evening hours. At about 4 o'clock yesterday afternoon, the court commission, consisting of District Judge Giessen, Medical Officer Dr. Med. Dreyfuss and the clerk arrived. At half past five the bodies were released and taken to the morgue. The store of Sidlin was judicially blocked. Immediately after the terrible act became public, an enormous crowd of people had accumulated on the streets, but they kept quiet. A large squad of police forces had to lock the road access.

We learn the following details about the personality of the murderer: Various signs suggest that Weise was in a state of mental disorder. The murderer received various postcards from Weise, which read dark incoherent words about the "nearness of the grave," the "angel of death" and so on. The illogical, incoherent style of writing suggests turbidity of the mental state. Weise also lived in strife in Dresden,

Newspaper article about the murder of Carl Sidlin: January 12, 1926 (English translation).

Todes-Anzeige

Gott dem. Ailtnächteges bat ei gentilzu. meinen lieben Mita.
ineienie ectugehezeine Kindes glücklichen Vater. eineeren I,,bin
Some. Sciiwi●grzoihri. Brirder und Schwager. Herrn

Carl Sidlin

IS ALter von 3t Jahren durch thettiOck ganz vierwartet zu tickt
in die Ewiqbett abzurufen.

lendeoelinhales a. MI.. Saarbrechen. Riga Vent, den II.
Januar 19.6

In heleier Iraner alle Ilinlicebbelenew

Wwe. Ibea Stdlin geb. Marx
und Xlereet

ni, It,eratig,,ng findet Mittwoch nachmittag 3 VW von *Au*
Sertebliicheti triedlonhalle toi statt- — Von kinaliplaika
rolle sen bitte sbeene●   4/3

Todes--Anzelge

Uneet bewahrtes. traute Mildbed. Herr

Carl Sidlin

Inhaber obart Goldwaseseschlites
nide leas *geeckt* denk den Tod sultaien-

St Ing **SNITIAIn 6111Aigill** a IS.
Mine**Duft 11011911-Clle M. 1. 1t**

Clan XIV (Rheimplals)

Di. Beritelairait zahl am Min woch. den 13. Januar
nachn Met 3 Uhr von ?ei Friedhofbete aus ;tett Wie
bi Cle● uniere fl.tgkgd,r uze rabliztibiolistenitgand

...bi. aast
Saal genees
● eneemetamsnemel●b●
SLUU143 zea. Wenq. e
e,lakiceterj - ta. Intab-
Coes" aelcoa
● lenkt te4).> all
hehe. eleteann ● verw.
V. swaccostigic.
0. *Itpieta*. ince, etre
ellenteeeen nenn
thestree *erqib* In
teI teeenett IL
Ciente 1. leab.
laihnen fre. alinete
nen-*So in..-*
tatitzeni● Sen

nebe tern Panel
aliteloqibe
CIL Mine sate
tok ei eek Senk

Carl Sidlin obituaries published in the newspaper: January 13, 1926 (Original in German).

Obituary

God the Almighty liked to call my dear husband, lucky father of our newborn child, our dear son, son-in-law, brother and brother-in-law, Mister

Carl Sidlin

at the age of 37 years unexpectedly by misfortune to eternity.

Ludwigshafen o. Rh., Saarbrücken, Riga, Paris, on January 11, 1926.

In deepest mourning bereaved:
Widow Thea Sidlin born Marx
and child.

The funeral will take place Wednesday afternoon at 3 o'clock, starting from the Israelite cemetery hall. -- Please refrain from wreath donations. 413

Obituary

Our established, faithful member, Mister   404

Carl Sidlin

Owner of a gold ware store
was unfortunately snatched from this life.

Automobile and Motorcycle Association
Ludwigshafen o. Rh.
General German Automobile Association (A. D. A. C.)
District XVI (Rheinpfalz)

The funeral will take place on Wednesday, January 13 at

Carl Sidlin obituaries published in the newspaper: January 13, 1926 (English translation).

Oskar and Terese's marriage certificate from the civil register. (Original in German)

No. *757*

(Notice of Intended Marriage Register No. *1374*)

Ludwigshafen on the Rhine, on _November twelfth nineteen_ hundred _twenty nine_.

Before the signed registrar appeared today for the purpose of marriage:

1. the _business man Abraham Herschel Oskar Schwarz, known in person_

The personality known as...

born on _October twenty seventh_
of the year _eighteen_ hundred _ninety one_
in _Przemysl, Galicia, now Poland,_   birth   register
No. _503_ of the registrar _in Israeliti Notariat's office in Przemysl._
Volume XVIII, page 207.

residing in _Berlin-Wilmersdorf Kaiserallee 176·_

2. the _business owner Therese Sidßn born Marx,_
widow, known in person

The personality known as...

born on _May twelfth_
of the year _nineteen_ hundred _____
in _Ralingen, administrative district Trier,_   birth register No.
_19_ of the birth register office _in Welschbillig, administrative district Trier,_

residing in _Ludwigshafen, Schanzstrasse 86;_

According to § 2 of the 2nd Ordinance on the Implementation of the Act on the Change of Surname and Given Names of August 17, 1938, the mentioned _Abraham Herschel Oskar Schwarz_ with effect from January 1st 1939 he has also adopted the additional first name _Israel._
Ludwigshafen on the Rhine, on _December 28th 1938_
The official registrar
By proxy

According to § 2 of the 2nd Ordinance on the Implementation of the Act on the Change of Surname and Given Names of August 17, 1938 the mentioned Therese _Schwarz_ born _Marx_ with effect from January 1st 1939 he has adopted the additional first name Sarah.
Ludwigshafen on the Rhine, on _December 28th 1938_
The official registrar
By proxy

Oskar and Terese's marriage certificate from the civil register. (English Translation)

Häftling

Vorname	ABRAHAM
Nachname	SCHWARZ
Geburtedatum	27.10.1891
Geburtsort	Przemysl
Wohnort	Ludwigshafen
Geschlecht	m
Beruf	Kaufmann
Konfession	israelitisch
Kinder	1
Quellenhinweis	NARA Zugangsbuch Nr. 105 / 25516
Zuletzt bekannte Zugangsstelle	-

Haftverlauf

Datum	Haftnummer	Haftländerung	Außenlager	Zu-/Abgangsstelle
12.11.1938	25539	Zugang		
20.12.1938	0	entlassen		

Haftkategorie

Jude: Schutzhäftling

Nationalität

Staatenlos

Quellen

Name	ITS 101 / 075

Oskar Schwarz internment certification at Dachau after Kristallnact.

L Schreiben an

neszn
Oscar /eraelSchwarz

begngstafen <u>an Rhein</u>
Trineregentenstr.

<u>Genen Zustellungsnachweist</u>

12; 88.A.s.　　　8.2.1939

am. * Ausschaltung der Juden aus den deutschen ',rtscheftsleben; hier
Auflösung und Abnicklang der JUlachen Einzelhandelsgeschäfte im
Stadkreis Ludwigshafen aa Rhein.

Gen Verordnung zur Ausschaltung cler Juden aus den•deutschien
Wirtechefsleben voe 12.11.38. und der Durchfithrungs-Verordsnng hierzu
voa 23411.38.₁ sowie der Runderlasse des Reiehswirtsclaaftaminiaers von
18.11.38. tesw. 25.11.38. ist Ehr Gewerbebetrieb aufzulösen und
abzuwickeln.

Die Abwicklung hat nach folgenden trundsätzen zu esfoi₊ren:
1) Der Vorkauf oder die Vereateligerung Ton Wesen tiat actszase ves-
breucher sind nicht zulässig.
2) Alls earen sind zunachst der zustandigen Fachgruppe oder
Zweckvereinigung oder deren bezirklicher oder fachlicher
Untergliederung anzubieten, die für die Unterbringung der Waren
Sorge zu tragen hat.
5) Die Fachgruppe oder Zweckvereinigung, der die vorhandenen
Waren zunikenst anzubieten sind, hat sich La eilen fIllen binnen
1a Tageft seit Singens; des Angebotes schriftlich zu äußern
und, falle sie ⅲₜₜ angebotenen Asten ,lieht unterbringen kann,
VerschlUge fUr eint anderweitig. sachifflae. Verwertung au
machen.
Erfolgt nach Ablauf de* Frist keins befriedigende Woherung der
lachgruppe oder Zbeckvereinigung, so ist Ule VerauAe-rung der
vorhandenen Werte zulässig.
4) Die Uebernehee der Weren erfolgt auf Grund einer Bewertung der isre
durca einen SacAverständi₊en.
• edie Senhverständige hat seine Bewertung nach kautsäenlachen
Grundsätzen vorzunehmen. Er soll dabei in erster Linie von des
einkaufepreis *der* vorhandenen Waren nuagehom und ist
berechtigt, In Fallen, in denen die "sie durch Zeitablauf oder
sonstige Umstands an Wert verloren hott, einen den
heutigen Umkaufswert entsprechendste Betrag festzusetzen.

Letter to Oskar telling him to dissolve the jewelry store, Feb 8, 1939. (Original in German)

I.   Letter to

Mister
Oskar Israel Schwarz

Ludwigshafen on the Rhein

Prinzregentenstr.

Proof of Delivery Requested

12; Sü./Wi.   Feb 8th1939

Subj.: Elimination of Jews from German economic life; here
        dissolution and settlement of the Jewish retail stores in the district
        of Ludwigshafen on the Rhine.

According to decree on the elimination of Jews from the German
economic life of November 12th 1938 and the implementing regulation thereto
of November 23rd 1938, as well as circular order of the Reich Minister of Economics of
November 18th 1938 and November 25th 1938 your business enterprise has to be dissolved
and handled.
        The settlement must be based on following instructions:

1)   The sale or auction of goods to final customers is forbidden.

2)   All goods must first be offered to the relevant trade group, association of
       interests or to their district or technical subdivision. They must arrange for
       the accommodation of the goods.

3)   The trade group or association of interests to which the existing goods were
       offered must in all cases provide written comments within 14 days of
       receiving the offer. If they cannot accommodate the offered goods, they need
       to make proposals for any other appropriate exploitation. If, after the expiry
       of the period, no satisfactory statement is made by the trade group or
       association of interests, the sale of the existing values is permitted.

4)   The goods are accepted on the basis of an evaluation of the wares by an expert.
       The expert has to carry out his evaluation in accordance with commercial
       principles. He shall primarily take the purchase price of the existing goods as a
       starting point and shall be entitled, in cases where the goods have lost value
       through time or other circumstances, to name a value according to the present
       purchase value.

Letter to Oskar telling him to dissolve the jewelry store, Feb 8, 1939. (English Translation)

```
     Gekar Schwarz, vorm.C.Sidlin
Lolwigehafen a. Sh.
Prierregestenetr. 6e.
```

```
                         Beiliegend isofetellung über wein Iaqerbeetaal
        ttr Sinheufewert von .K. 2874.45
                         MIO treferanren sind folgende t.
```

```
Fa. Gebr. Sunqeana. Sekramberq
•    Serwann Sekweiter,   .
     leurteänqler Söhne, fortesuen.
     Kieez/e, Schwenainses
•    Stneen & Spann, Mim
     Gebr, Mähler, Stuttqart
•    Brwin Lenz,
•    Karl Ekbwann, Pforzheim
•    orsos Schwenaissen
     1. Kling, Ulmnhelm
•    Mas, Nenaketm
•    Schock & Frank, Sehwäb. Gmünd
     Sdnerä Lohe , Stuttqart
     Lehnnne & CO, Pfonkeln
•    Äuq. Hilles, öberetelm
     Plune. Berlin
•    Spuckmalm & Söhne, Beilbronn
•    ehrtteeberqische Metallwarenfabrik, Geielinsen
•    geiet, Seeliesen
•    gl. Deetjen, Freudenstadt.
```

yed,e2, Zeste24/

LedeigAtafell it. Rh. 10.2.39.

Inventory of the store done by Oskar after getting the letter to shut down the store.

Kaufvertrag

Zwischen

Herrn Oekar Israel Schwarz. labreachermeleter,
   Iadelgehafen (2bein), Prinzregentenstr. 68

und

Herrn Karl Schenk, Wutzlaehermeister,
   Ludeigahafen (Rhein), Ereobigebetr. 12

wird heute folgender Vertrag abgeschlossen,

3 1

Herr Schwarz verkauft an iioXtri Schenk folgende
Gegenständes

a) deo gement. Warenlager, lt. besonderer, dem
    Gewerbeamt Indeigahafen (Rhein) eingereichter
    Liste, ineboomdere aber die Waren, die eicht in
    der Liste aufgefährt sind, die noch In Geschäft
    und Werketatt vorhanden sind.

b) sämtliche in den Läden-, Geschäfts- und Heller-
    räumen der trUheren Fixum 0. J. Schwan befind-
    liehen 3inriebtunge- und sonstigen Gegenstände,
    soweit sie nicht Zigenten &es Hausbeoitters sind.

Als Kaufpreie wird rar sämtliche in '5 1 festgelegten
Gegenstände

Distressed sales contract of the jewelry store to Karl Schenk. (Original in German)

S a l e s Agreement

between

Mister Oskar Israel Schwarz, master watchmaker,
        Ludwigshafen (Rhine), Prinzregentenstr. 68

and

Mister Karl Schenk, master watchmaker,
        Ludwigshafen (Rhine). Brechlochstr. 12

the following contract will be concluded today:

§ 1

Mister Schwarz sells to Mister Schenk the following
items:

a) the entire warehouse, according to a special list submitted to
   the official trade office Ludwigshafen (Rhein).
   Particularly the goods though that are not
   listed in the list, but can still be found in the business room
   and workshop.

b) all furnishings and other items stored in the store rooms, business rooms and cellars of
   the former company O. J. Schwarz, unless they are the property of the homeowner.

§ 2

The purchase price for all items listed in § 1 were set to

. / .

Distressed sales contract of the jewelry store to Karl Schenk. (English Translation)

USTE DES CONVOIS DE JUR

LIST OF THE CONIVOYS OF JEWS DEPORTEC

DAIE DE DSPARI	N• DU CONVOI	UEU DU ITS5 PART	DESTINATON	NOMBRE DE DIPORT/S AU CAMP DE DESTINATION Re60.¹11	GA2I5 À UARINVEE	SItiCTIONNIS À AUSCHWITZ FEMMES	St HOM2
1942							
27.03	1		CPAIICIiC01915YGNE	1 112		1112	
05 06	2		C0121¹402NE	7 000		1 000	
22 06	3	019417/C3	MACNRATZ	COO		933	06
25 06	4		0113150C05	991		1 000	
28 0.1	5		84/11/NE344904ANDE	1 03A		1 004	-14
1707	6		snisems ne			80/	110
1907	)		CWANCV	999	375	604	171
20 01	8	ANGERS	AUX111612	877	23	.411	
22 07	9	DOANCY	4115011172	996		615	385
24 07	10	O1ANCY	AUSON7117	1 000		373	630
27.07	11	DRANCY	AKneffeen	.CO		248	742
sei»	12	DRANCY	MECK 492	:001	216	270	514
3107	13	PIiHNIERS	AU1011192	1 049		993	350 -
0301	M	1110123	AUSCHWII	1 034	482	22	$17 •
• D5 08	15	817ª01(4490l4101	AUSCHWTZ	1 014	104	2¼	98
0701	16	PreFfseR5	AUSCHAITZ	1 010	7,4	63	211
08	C	ORANCY	AUSCHWITZ	1 036	768	140	100
12 011	18	DRANCY	AUSCHWITZ	1207	705	203	62
14 08	10	DM/10Y	AUSCHWITZ	991	875	115	
17GS	20	DRANCY	AUSCHWITZ	000	ela	65	34
19 04	21	DRAHOI	AUSCHWITZ	000	all	ISS	451
21 08	22	DRANCY	AUSCHWITZ	000	192	901	
24 03	22	DRANC9	AUSCHWITZ	003	908	92	
2608	24	1524313,		032	937	27	36	21
2808	25	011ANCY	AUSOMITZ	0011	929		71	8•
31 el	29	D9ANCY	POSeffmte	070	961	12	9?	16
02 CO	27	DRANG,	MISCH3²/117	070	777	10	113	30
04 09	28	011ANCY	AUSCHWITZ	013	959	16		595
0709	29	09ANCY	Att1Ctiverz	090	101	59	52	ad
0909	30	0441/0	meadwre	000	909	st	11	al
107	31	(JRANO)	AMdeal	003	420	2	78	13
14 1P)	32	D11910)	403011¹41Z	000	113	58	49	Ae
I909	13	01141445¹	me.Can	003	844			37
1/1 CO	31	041ANCV	AUSCHAM	010	869	31	110	22
21 09	36	MWAIRS		003	nt	14		29
2301	39	IWANCT	AUSCHWTZ	000	475	349	133	21
25 01	31	011ANO	AUSCHWTZ	004	173		91	10
28 01	34	0941400	AUSCHWT1	904	733	123		20
30 09	39	00ANCV	AUSCHWYZ	210	154	34	23	0
UH	03	047411C¹¹	AUSCHATZ	1000	639	269	92	4
0411	42	DOANCY	411300192	e00	733	145	23	4
0011	44		0491410i	1 030	900		103	
11 11	46	D041¹4CY	AUSCHWYZ' L	746	898	112	34	2

41 COnvolt sont perliS 07 la qane du noureet (27 m8,6723 NN **1543**)
ol 21 CnIettiat da na aa,,a itakms• Im ;42earili Atta testi

Deportation convoys from France while Charles was living in France.

Charles living facilities in Switzerland, Oct 1942 – Sep 1945		
Facility	Start date	End date
Stade de Varande (Varande Stadium), Geneva	04 Oct 1942	13 Oct 1942
Heiden	13 Oct 1942	20 Oct 1942
Home for Refugee Children Administration, Waldeck, Langenbruck	20 Oct 1942	10 May 1943
Labor Camp for internee Arisdorf	10 May 1943	11 Jul 1943
Children's Sanatorium Basel, Langenbruck	11 Jul 1943	15 Nov 1943
Labor Camp Davesco, Tessin	15 Nov 1943	22 Jun 1944
Les Murailles Children's Home, Vesenaz (Geneva)	22 Jun 1944	22 Jan 1945
Aliah de la Jeunesse Home, Pont-Céard, Versoix	22 Jan 1945	06 Apr 1945
Home Beau Sejour, Geneva	06 Apr 1945	15 Jun 1945
Hotel Beaujolais, Geneva	15 Jun 1945	Sep 1945

Charles Living Facilities in Switzerland, Oct 1942 – Sep 1945

Eidg. Justiz- und Polizeidepartement
POLIZEIABTEILUNG

N 11709 Jf

Bern, den 8. Dezember 1943

An die
Leitung des Arbeitslagers
für Internierte,
D a v e s c o ./Tessin.

Wir beziehen uns auf das Gesuch des bei Ihnen internierten **Flüchtlings Karl S c h w a r z** , geb. 4. Januar 1926 vom **29. November 1943** und teilen Ihnen mit, dass wir die Schweizerische Volksbank in Bern beauftragt haben, Ihnen aus dem betreffenden Depotkonto

den Betrag von Fr. 50.— anzuweisen. **(Fünfzig)**

Wir bitten Sie, **Karl Schwarz** Dieses Geld auszuhändigen und zu überwachen, dass es für den im Gesuch angegebenen Zweck verwendet wird.

Weitere Bemerkungen:
Anschaffungen.

Mit vorzüglicher Hochachtung
DER CHEF DER POLIZEIABTEILUNG
i... **sig. Fehlmann**

Kopie an die Schweizerische Volksbank, Bern, mit der Bitte um Anweisung des Betrages.
F 90 d   hu

Response from police to Charles' request for 50 Swiss franc reimbursement in December 1943 (Original in German).

Conf. Justice and Police Department
POLICE DIVISION   Bern, on 8. December 1943

N 11709 Jf

To the
**Administration of Labor Camps
for Internee,
Davesco./Tessin.**

We refer to the petition of **November 29, 1943** concerning the interned **refugee Karl Schwarz, b. January 4,1926,** and inform you that we have instructed the Swiss Volksbank in Bern to instruct to pay you from the custody account

the amount of CHF **50.- (Fifty).**

We ask that you hand over this money to **Karl Schwarz** and monitor that it is used for the purpose stated in the request.

Further remarks:
Purchases.

With great respect
CHIEF OF THE POLICE DEPARTMENT
p. p. **sig. Fehlmann**

Copy to the Swiss Volksbank, Bern, with a request for allocation of the amount.

F 90 d

Response from police to Charles' request for 50 Swiss franc reimbursement in December 1943 (English translation).

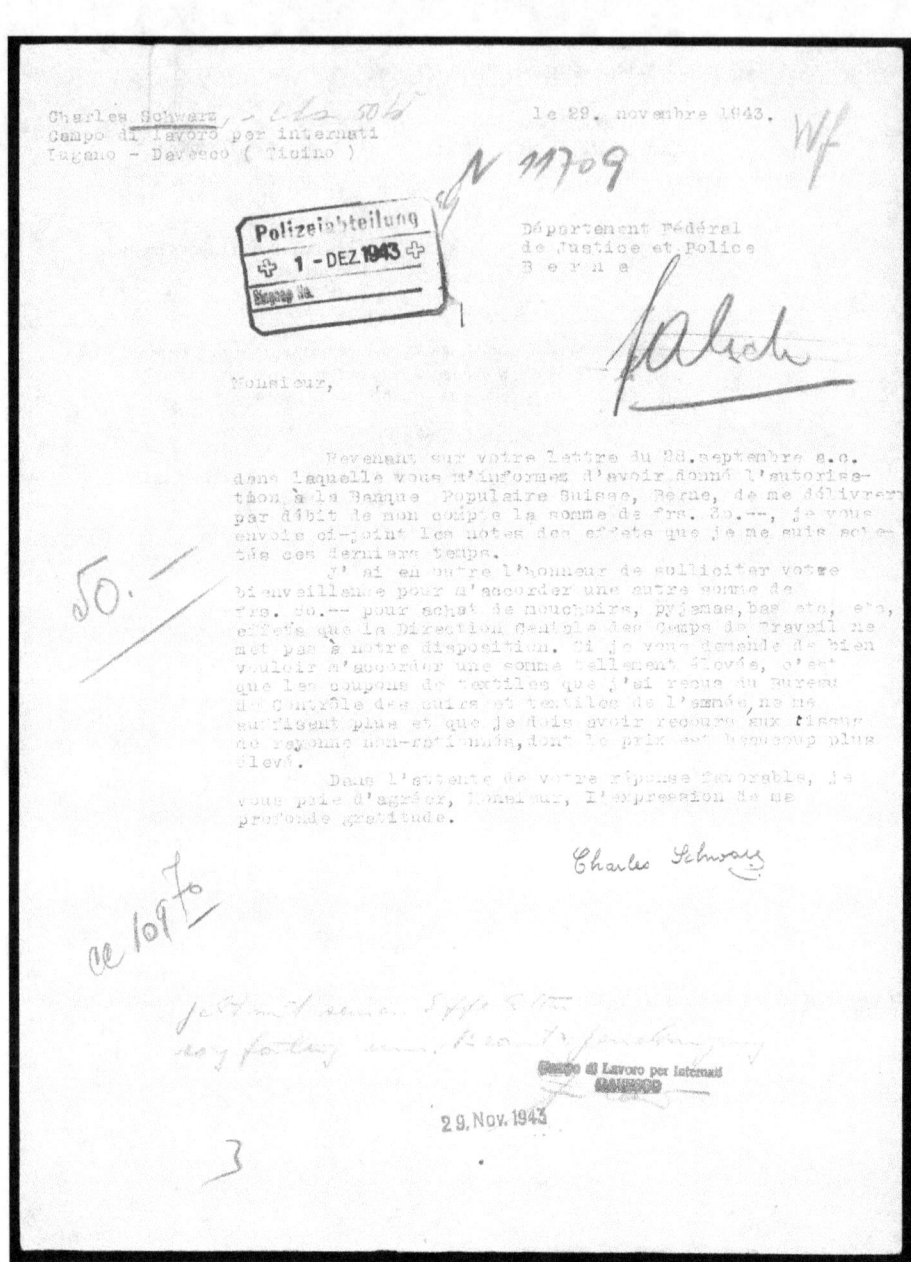

Charles' request to the police for 80 franc reimbursement for the purchase of tissues, socks, pajamas, November 1943 (Original in German).

Charles Schwarz
1943 Camp di lavoro, per internati

November 29th,

Federal Department
of Justice and Police
Berne

Sir,

As per your letter dated September 28th, in which I was informed that an authoraization was given to the Banque Populaire Suisse, Bern, to debit my account for the sum of 30 francs-, I send you, herewith, the notes stating the effects which I have recently purchased.

In addition, I have the honor to solicit your kindness in granting an additional amount of 80 francs – for the purchase of tissues, pyjamas, socks etc., etc. items that the Central Management of Labor Camps do not put at our disposal. If I ask for such a large amount, it is because the textile coupons received by the Army's Leather and Textile Office do not suffice and I have to resort to using non-rationed rayon tissue, which is much more expensive.

Looking forward to your favorable response, please accept, my deepest gratitude.

Charles Schwarz

Charles' request to the police for 80 franc reimbursement for the purchase of tissues, socks, pajamas, November 1943 (English translation).

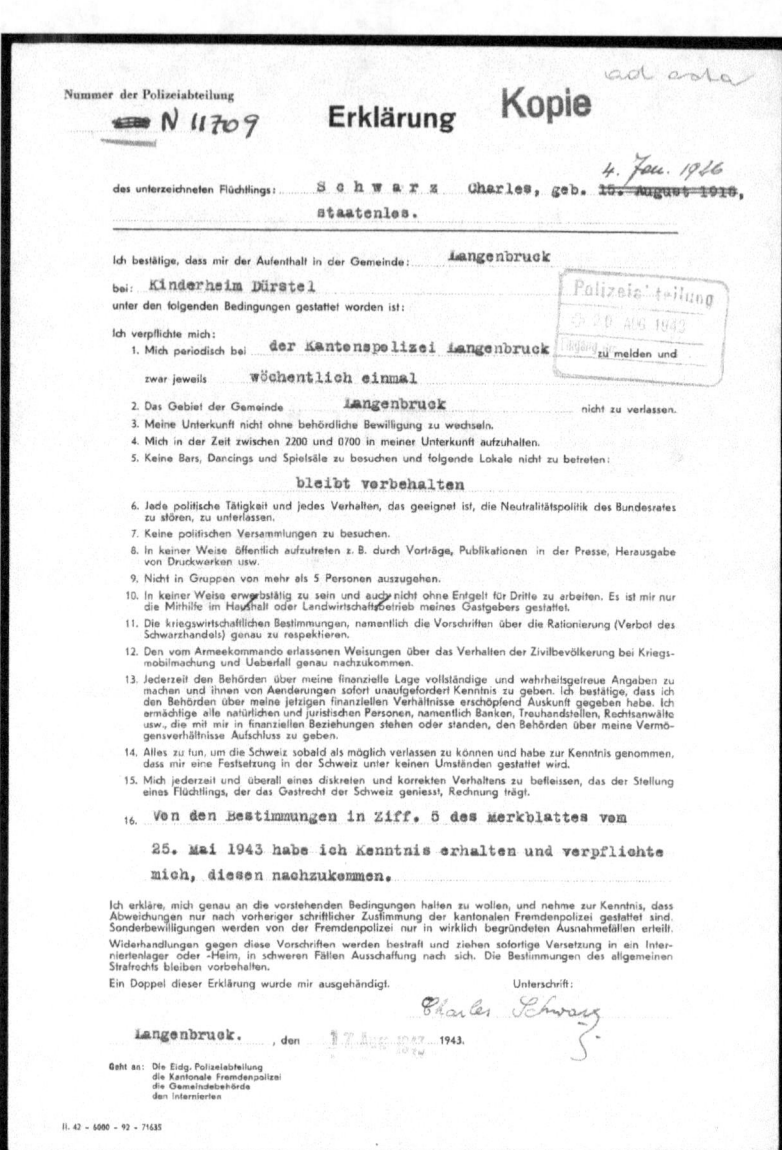

Nummer der Polizeiabteilung

N 11709   **Erklärung**   **Kopie**   *ad acta*

des unterzeichneten Flüchtlings: S c h w a r z   Charles, geb. ~~15. August 1916~~,   *4. Jan. 1916*

staatenlos.

Ich bestätige, dass mir der Aufenthalt in der Gemeinde: Langenbruck

bei: Kinderheim Dürstel

unter den folgenden Bedingungen gestattet worden ist:

Ich verpflichte mich:

1. Mich periodisch bei   der Kantonspolizei Langenbruck   zu melden und

    zwar jeweils   wöchentlich einmal

2. Das Gebiet der Gemeinde   Langenbruck   nicht zu verlassen.
3. Meine Unterkunft nicht ohne behördliche Bewilligung zu wechseln.
4. Mich in der Zeit zwischen 2200 und 0700 in meiner Unterkunft aufzuhalten.
5. Keine Bars, Dancings und Spielsäle zu besuchen und folgende Lokale nicht zu betreten:

    bleibt vorbehalten

6. Jede politische Tätigkeit und jedes Verhalten, das geeignet ist, die Neutralitätspolitik des Bundesrates zu stören, zu unterlassen.
7. Keine politischen Versammlungen zu besuchen.
8. In keiner Weise öffentlich aufzutreten z. B. durch Vorträge, Publikationen in der Presse, Herausgabe von Druckwerken usw.
9. Nicht in Gruppen von mehr als 5 Personen auszugehen.
10. In keiner Weise erwerbstätig zu sein und auch nicht ohne Entgelt für Dritte zu arbeiten. Es ist mir nur die Mithilfe im Haushalt oder Landwirtschaftsbetrieb meines Gastgebers gestattet.
11. Die kriegswirtschaftlichen Bestimmungen, namentlich die Vorschriften über die Rationierung (Verbot des Schwarzhandels) genau zu respektieren.
12. Den vom Armeekommando erlassenen Weisungen über das Verhalten der Zivilbevölkerung bei Kriegsmobilmachung und Ueberfall genau nachzukommen.
13. Jederzeit den Behörden über meine finanzielle Lage vollständige und wahrheitsgetreue Angaben zu machen und ihnen von Aenderungen sofort unaufgefordert Kenntnis zu geben. Ich bestätige, dass ich den Behörden über meine jetzigen finanziellen Verhältnisse erschöpfend Auskunft gegeben habe. Ich ermächtige alle natürlichen und juristischen Personen, namentlich Banken, Treuhandstellen, Rechtsanwälte usw., die mit mir in finanziellen Beziehungen stehen oder standen, den Behörden über meine Vermögensverhältnisse Aufschluss zu geben.
14. Alles zu tun, um die Schweiz sobald als möglich verlassen zu können und habe zur Kenntnis genommen, dass mir eine Festsetzung in der Schweiz unter keinen Umständen gestattet wird.
15. Mich jederzeit und überall eines diskreten und korrekten Verhaltens zu befleissen, das der Stellung eines Flüchtlings, der das Gastrecht der Schweiz geniesst, Rechnung trägt.
16. Von den Bestimmungen in Ziff. 5 des Merkblattes vom

    25. Mai 1943 habe ich Kenntnis erhalten und verpflichte

    mich, diesen nachzukommen.

Ich erkläre, mich genau an die vorstehenden Bedingungen halten zu wollen, und nehme zur Kenntnis, dass Abweichungen nur nach vorheriger schriftlicher Zustimmung der kantonalen Fremdenpolizei gestattet sind. Sonderbewilligungen werden von der Fremdenpolizei nur in wirklich begründeten Ausnahmefällen erteilt.

Widerhandlungen gegen diese Vorschriften werden bestraft und ziehen sofortige Versetzung in ein Interniertenlager oder -Heim, in schweren Fällen Ausschaffung nach sich. Die Bestimmungen des allgemeinen Strafrechts bleiben vorbehalten.

Ein Doppel dieser Erklärung wurde mir ausgehändigt.

Unterschrift: *Charles Schwarz*

Langenbruck.   , den   17 Aug 1943   1943.

Geht an: Die Eidg. Polizeiabteilung
die Kantonale Fremdenpolizei
die Gemeindebehörde
den Internierten

II. 42 – 6000 – 92 – 71635

Document signed by Charles in every city he lived in Switzerland agreeing to the terms of his refugee status.(Original in German.)

ad acta

copy

Number of Police Department	
4168 N 11709	**Statement**

4. Jan. 1926

Signing refugee: Schwarz Charles, born 15 August 1915
stateless.

I confirm to have been granted a stay in the municipal: **Langenbruck**

at: **Children's home Dürstel**
under the following conditions:

Police Department
• 20 AUG. 1943 •

I obligate myself:

1.

namely

    to periodically check in with the
    Cantonal Police Langenbruck

    twice a week

   2.   Not to leave the area of the municipal:
        Langenbruck
   3.   Not to change my accommodation does without official permission.
   4.   To stay in my accommodation between 10 pm and 7 am.
        subject to change

   5.   To refrain from any political activity or behavior that is capable of disrupting the Federal
       Council's policy of neutrality.
   4.   Not to visit any political meetings.
   5.   Not to perform publicly in any way through for example lectures, publications in the press,
       publication of printed matter, etc.
   6.   Not to go out in groups of 5 or more people.
   7.   To not being gainfully employed and not working for a third party without pay. I am only
       allowed to assist in the home or farm of my host.
   8.   To strictly respect the provisions of the war economy, namely the rules on rationing
       (prohibition of trafficking).
   9.   To comply exactly with the instructions issued by the Army Command on the behavior of the
       civilian population in the mobilization and assault of war.
   10. At any time to give the authorities full and accurate information about my financial situation
       and to inform them immediately of any changes. I confirm that I have given the authorities
       exhaustive information about my current financial situation. I authorize all natural and legal
       persons, including banks, fiduciaries, lawyers, etc., who have or are in financial relationships
       with me, to inform the authorities of my financial circumstances.
   11. To do everything to be able to leave Switzerland as soon as possible and have taken note that
       under no circumstances will I be allowed to be bound in Switzerland.
   12. To use at any time and everywhere a discrete and correct attitude that takes into account the
       position of a refugee enjoying Switzerland's right of residence.
   13. I have received knowledge of the provisions in section 5 of the leaflet of 25 May 1943
       and undertake to comply with them.

    I declare that I want to abide by the above conditions and note that deviations are only permitted after prior
written consent of the cantonal aliens police. Special permits are issued by the immigration authorities only in
really justified exceptional cases.
    Violations of these rules will be punished and will result in immediate transfer to an interned camp or interned
home, in serious cases deportation. The provisions of general criminal law remain reserved.
A duplicate of this statement was given to me.

              Langenbruck, on 17. August 1943

goes in: Confederate Police Department Cantonale Immigration Authorities Local Authorities Internat	Signature: *Charles Schwarz*

Document signed by Charles in every city he lived in Switzerland agreeing to the terms of his refugee status.(English translation)

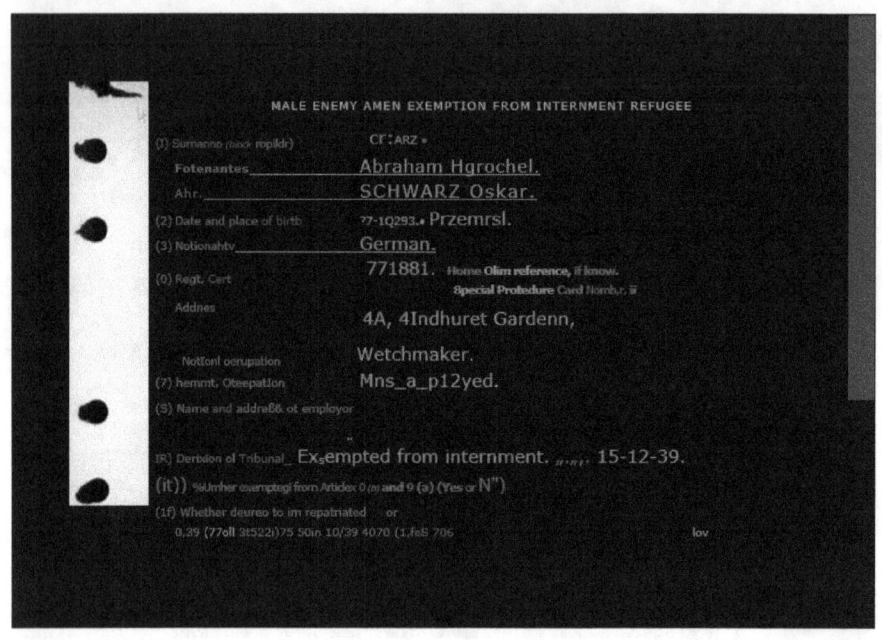

Certificate of exemption for Oskar from internment for refugees in England.

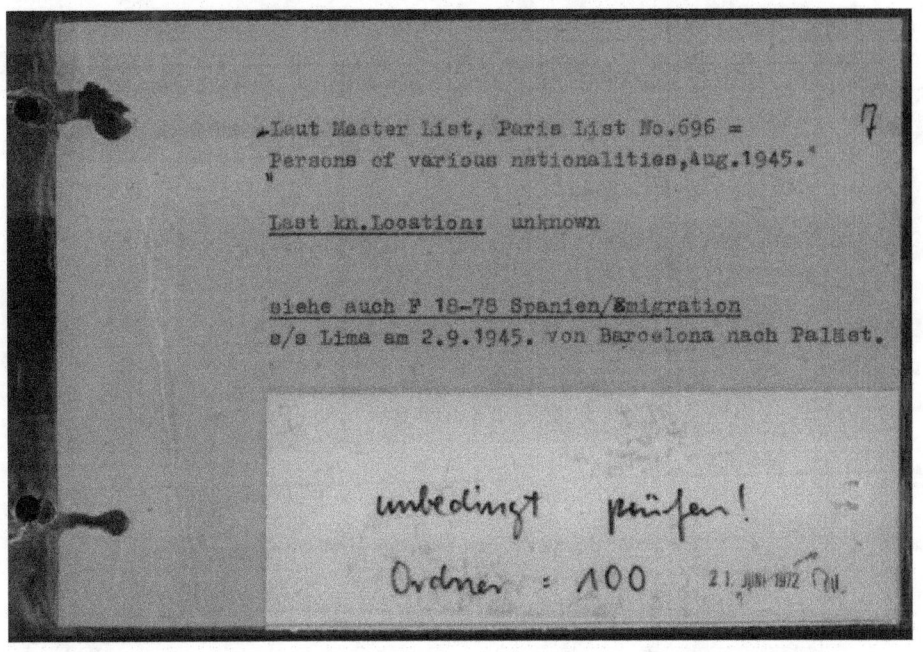

List of passengers sailing from Barcelona to Palestine, September 1945.

Name: 5 CILWAR TZ, Clmrles

BD: ^{19} J • **BP:** go nociAy **Nat:** doutoch

List Ot LWtierante arrived in Paleettito on 11,9.1945 from • PrItiou on board of S/S "LM". Patherl a Molt)lor e NaMOS • tel Oskar, • Teresa Lfd$_e$lio.1　265.	urholten vom 7130 London ~~CMM~~ ta IP 18 - 50 P8lU8ttM

Ship manifest stating Charles' arrival in Palestine from Barcelona. (Original in German)

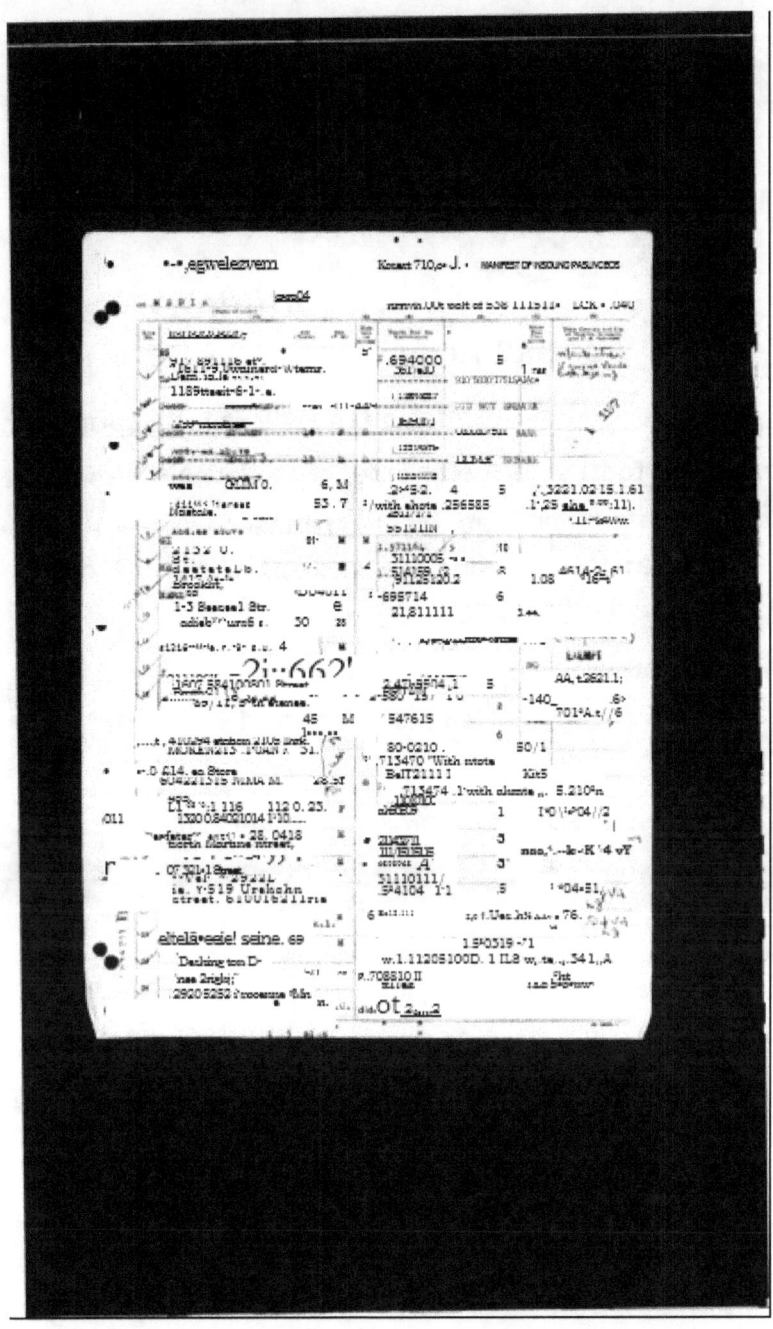

Ship manifest for Charles' sailing from Liverpool to New York.

No. 7000097

Name   SCHURZ Amleo

ᵢuiding ot   **110-28 Zet h 8t Laure ton**

Date of **airtgan 1^1 9^{26}** Mar order of admistiooNOV.·3199

Date unifeste immed $30^1$1%-1371952 ---------------- bY the

    U. Diatriet   c$_o$ur$t$ ot BrooktnkNow York

Petition **No/^{97}.,-;** $\nearrow$

Mien Registration   , A

       Z o t e h t e i t o : 4 $_d$

          and 1mme   ʋʋɾʎ»

Charles Schwarz Naturalization Card in the USA

_No._ 7376240 is

Name   SCHWiLLiZ ʟ. Therese

residing at_ 79aRiveraide_ _Dr>_ _ NI_ --
         May 12, 1900   Nov 11 1954
Date of birth---------------------- Date of order of admission -------------------

Date certificate issued Nov., 11 1954   by thi

     U. S. District   Court at New York aty, New York

Petition No. 610517

Alien RegistTation NEE 7 172 621

(Compkte and true signaturzgₑekimt----…

Terese Schwarz Naturalization Card in the USA

105

fh

N$_o$. 7505050

Name	SCHURZ Oskar

residing of **790 Riverside Drive,** titelt Ygork i Ns

October 27, 1891 !Key 18, 1955

Date of birth-------------------- Date of order of admission-------------------

Date certificate issued	Mv 16$_t$ 1955		by th

U. S. District	Court at **New York City, New York**

Petition No._ ' _C2 *39.5*

Allen Registration No.	7 174 688
	(Complete and true signature of holder)

Charles Schwarz Naturalization Card in the USA

Consultant
Schuler, attorney
District Court Neustadt/W'str.
-/- district Court Zweibrücken
-/- (22b) Zweibrücken
-/- mailbox 53 – call 2545
-/- account Ludwigshafen 1392

O (W9/452/59 now 673/60

Zweibrücken, on 29-May 1959

CHARGE for

S C H W A R Z Oskar, born on 27-October 1891, New York 32, N. Y. U.S.A, 790 Riverside
Drive, represented by attorney consultant Schuler in Zweibrücken, plaintiff.

against

the District Rhineland-Pfalz, represented by the warden of the state agency for reparations
and agency funds, defendants.

The district agency for reparations in Neustadt / Weinstrasse issued under the file number
193 393R, serial number E 1221/58 on 8th December 1958 a decision E (II / 7a), which
was received from at the time representative of the plaintiff, Hermann Marx in Paris, 33
rue Doudeauville on 11th December 1958.

The decision states that the plaintiff is entitled to capital compensation amounting to
DM 15,768.- until December 31, 1948, but beyond that he is not entitled to a pension,
since he had returned to his former income by 1 January 1949.

In the attachment I hand over the power of attorney signed by the plaintiff and raise
against the above-mentioned notice of determination

CHARGE

with the request to award the plaintiff a monthly pension for the period from 1 January
1949 until his death, the amount of which shall be at the discretion of the court, but at
least DM 540.- per month, as determined by the District Office for Reparations; as well
as to decide about the legal costs of the lawsuit.

*First page of complaint filed by Oskar for reparations paid as a lifetime
pension.(English translation)*

Larry (left) and Ron (right) after the stolpersteine installation. The 3 installed stones are shown in front.

Charles at La Guette, circa 1940

Back row: Charles and Oskar
Front row: Gerry and Terese
In NY at Oskar & Terese apartment
Circa 1951

www.ingramcontent.com/pod-product-compliance
Lightning Source LLC
Chambersburg PA
CBHW060939120626
46557CB00003B/1067